Teacher's Guide

Basic English Grammar

Bonnie L. Walker

AGS®
American Guidance Service
4201 Woodland Road
Circle Pines, Minnesota 55014-1796

Staff

Barbara Pokrinchak, Ed.D., Executive Editor
Beth C. Hornung, Editor
Norm Myers, Design Services

ISBN: 0-86601-959-6

Order Number: 80011

A 9 8 7 6 5 4 3 2

CONTENTS

Teacher's Guide
to
BASIC ENGLISH GRAMMAR

Introduction

Basic English Grammar is divided into two parts. Part 1 is titled Grammar and Usage. Students will learn the eight parts of speech and their usage in sentences. Each chapter in Part 1 deals with one part of speech. Capitalization, spelling, and punctuation are introduced within each lesson as these skills relate to the grammatical structures that are presented.

Part 2 is titled Sentence Structure. Students will learn each type of sentence used in spoken English. Part 2 presents sentence structures including simple, compound, and complex sentences. Students will analyze and practice each pattern.

Each part is organized into chapters, lessons, and activities. Each lesson highlights one aspect of the chapter topic. At least one activity is included for each grammar rule, variation of a rule, or concept that is introduced.

Each chapter begins with a series of Warm-Up exercises that may be used as a diagnostic activity or pretest. All chapters and lessons end with a Lesson Review, which covers the rules and concepts presented. These review activities may be used to determine if the student has mastered the material in that section.

Reading Level

The reading level in the text has been determined to be at a level of 2.6 (Spache). The variables of sentence length, sentence structure, and vocabulary have been controlled in all aspects of content, including explanations, examples, and activities.

In addition to words considered by the author to be difficult, this *Teacher's Guide* lists by lesson all words classified above the fourth grade level according to A *Revised Core Vocabulary* by Stanford E. Taylor, Helen Frackenpohl, and Catherine E. White. Grade levels for most of the vocabulary

words are indicated in parentheses. Nongraded words have no numerical designation.

The Teacher's Guide

This *Teacher's Guide* is designed to extend the concepts presented in the textbook. Each chapter is divided into lessons. Each lesson begins with an overview, and lesson goals and vocabulary words are listed. Teaching suggestions are recommended for mastering the chapter and lesson goals.

The Follow-Up activities can be used to augment individual lessons or to test the students' ability to retain what they have learned. This process will enable the teacher to spot any trouble areas and sharpen the students' proficiency.

The Student Workbook

A *Student Workbook* is available to supplement the textbook activities. Students having a difficult time grasping a particular concept will find this most helpful.

There are a minimum of three activities per chapter, with most chapters having five additional activities. These can be used as class tests, oral review, or homework. The student needing supplemental help can only benefit from this workbook. Answers are given beginning on page 81 of this *Teacher's Guide*.

Blackline Masters

A collection of reproducible *Blackline Masters* is also available. There are three activities per chapter with Mastery Tests after Part 1: Grammar and Usage and Part 2: Sentence Structure. The Mastery Tests cover all the material studied up to that point and evaluate whether or not the chapter goals have been met and accomplished.

The *Blackline Masters* can be used for a variety of purposes including class tests, oral review, and homework. Answers are given beginning on page 87 of this *Teacher's Guide*.

Part 1
Grammar and Usage

Overview
Part One consists of nine chapters. One part of speech, including concepts, rules, and usage is addressed in each chapter.

Chapter Goals
At the conclusion of Part 1, students are expected to:
- Identify the part of speech of every word in sample sentences.
- Provide correct parts of speech wherever needed in sample sentences.
- Rewrite incorrect sentences using correct parts of speech.
- Determine the grammatical accuracy of selected sentences.

Vocabulary

arrange (3)	italics (6)
arrangement (4)	language (4)
capitalize (9)	pronounce (4)
capitalization	pronunciation (5)
emphasize (7)	punctuation (7)
error (6)	rearrange
graduate (6)	usage (10)
grammar (5)	communicate (6)

Teaching Suggestions
1. Discuss the information provided on page 3 of the text.
2. Have students skim through the entire text. Point out the chapter structure, rules, reviews, and index.
3. Discuss the objectives for Part 1 so the students are aware of what they will be learning.
4. Incorporate the words in the vocabulary list in your instruction. Locate the words in the text and discuss them with the students.
5. Have the students do the activities. Discuss these activities with the entire group.

Follow-Up Activities
1. Have each student write a short sentence. Mix up the words and put the scrambled sentences on the chalkboard for the students to rearrange.
2. Give the students a topic, such as a current popular film, a television program, or a local landmark. Then, have the students write a short sentence about the topic. Put the sentences on the chalkboard. Ask the group to try to identify the part of speech for each word in the sentences. Then, have the group try to identify and correct any usage errors they find.

Answer Key for Introduction to Part 1
Pages 3-6
Activity A
1. Jack graduated from high school in June.
2. Manuel went on a vacation.
3. Mike listened to a new band.

Activity B
Sentences 1 and 3 are questions. (The words *do* and *is* at the beginning of the sentence are clues.) Sentence 2 is a statement.

Activity C
1. looked
2. fishing?"
3. Wednesday
4. He
5. Joe
6. knew

Activity D
1. Charlie and I
2. have already gone
3. himself
4. doesn't
5. We boys
6. any sense
7. gave

Activity E
1. adjective
2. noun
3. verb
4. conjunction
5. adverb
6. pronoun
7. preposition
8. verb
9. interjection

Chapter 1
The Noun

Overview

Chapter 1 is divided into three lessons. Lesson 1 develops the concept that nouns are words that name any person or thing. Lessons 2 and 3 focus on proper nouns and capitalization, plural nouns, and possessives.

Chapter Goals

At the conclusion of Chapter 1, students are expected to:
- recognize nouns in sentences;
- distinguish between proper and common nouns and to capitalize proper nouns;
- distinguish between singular and plural nouns and to write plural forms correctly;
- distinguish between plural nouns and possessives and to write each correctly.

Teaching Suggestions

1. Discuss the information given in the overview.
2. Discuss the objectives for the chapter.
3. Read the introductory text with the students. Have them complete the chapter Warm-Up independently; then discuss the correct answers.

Lesson 1. Finding Nouns in Sentences
Overview

Lesson 1 begins with activities designed to help students recognize nouns. Compound nouns (e.g., sunflower) and noun phrases (e.g., ice cream, son-in-law) are explained; concrete and abstract nouns are compared. There are also several activities to help students distinguish between nouns that name general things and nouns that are names of a certain or specific thing. Rules for proper nouns that are names of places, abbreviations, parts of the country, languages, courses, and titles are included.

Lesson Goals

At the conclusion of Lesson 1, students are expected to:
- identify nouns in sentences;
- distinguish between common and proper nouns;
- capitalize proper nouns in sentences.

Vocabulary

abbreviate (8)	direction (3)
abbreviation (8)	example (3)
abstract (9)	hyphen (6)
address (3)	insurance
agent (5)	interest (3)
appointment (6)	mileage (7)
capitalize (9)	part-time
certain (3)	policy (7)
common (3)	post office
compound (6)	proper
concrete (5)	protection (4)
course (3)	route (3)
coverage	subject (3)
decision (5)	title (5)

Teaching Suggestions

1. Discuss the lesson overview.
2. Discuss the lesson goals.
3. Only three words — abbreviate, abbreviation, and capitalize — are difficult words; however, students should review the entire vocabulary list before starting the lesson activities.
4. Do Activities B and C orally with the class to be sure the students understand the concept of names for certain or specific things, persons, and places.

Follow-Up Activities

1. Have the students describe a car that they would like to own. Tell them to write several sentences in a vertical list. Then, have them underline all of the nouns in their sentences. Ask for volunteers to read their sentences.
2. Explain to the class that one name for you is *teacher*. Another name is Mr. or Ms. _____. Have them think of other names by which you might be known, such as *friend, neighbor, sister/brother, aunt/uncle, student, driver*, etc.
3. Divide the class into two groups of teams. Write these words on the chalkboard: *school, city, sofa, car*. Have members of each team take turns writing "other names" for those nouns under each one listed. Allow each person a certain amount of time (about 20 seconds). The team that produces the most nouns is the winner.

4. Provide a list of the two-letter state abbreviations. After an oral review, call the state names and have the students practice writing the abbreviations. Then, give the students a list of abbreviations and have them identify the states.
5. Select a brief passage from a literature book, newspaper, or magazine. Have the students find and list the nouns. Then, have them divide the word into two groups: proper nouns and common nouns.

Lesson 2. Singular and Plural Nouns
Overview
Lesson 2 develops the concepts of singular and plural nouns. The activities stress pronunciation and hearing the difference between the singular and plural forms. Plurals that are irregular in form are included. Forming plurals is an especially difficult problem for students. These drills are well worth the time involved. Encourage frequent use of the dictionary.

Lesson Goals
At the conclusion of the lesson, the students are expected to:
• Identify nouns in sentences;
• Write the plural form of regular and irregular nouns;
• Identify plural nouns in sentences.

Vocabulary
community college (5.5)	plural (6)
celebrate (4)	preparation (4)
form (3)	regular (4)
irregular (7)	singular (8)
memorize (6)	syllable (4)
misspelled	

Teaching Suggestions
1. Discuss the information in the overview.
2. Discuss the lesson goals.
3. Read the introductory paragraph carefully.
4. Use the vocabulary list as part of your instruction.
5. Do Activity C orally with the class. Other activities in Lesson 2 are suitable for independent practice.

Follow-Up Activities
1. Have the students write a few sentences about a party they have given or attended, listing the sentences vertically. Then have them find and underline all of the plural nouns that they have written. They should check the spelling of the plural forms.
2. Make a concentration game with 26 index cards cut in half (52 cards). On the cards, write 26 singular nouns and their matching 26 plural forms. Include deer or sheep (written the same way on both cards) and other irregular plural nouns. To play the game, Player 1 turns over two cards. If they match, the player has a pair and turns over two more cards. If they do not match, Player 2 takes a turn. The player with the most pairs wins. Encourage frequent use of the dictionary.

Lesson 3. Nouns That Are Possessive
Overview
In Lesson 3, students learn about the singular and plural possessive forms of the noun. Because plurals and possessives sound the same when spoken, mastering the possessive is probably the most difficult skill that the students will be asked to accomplish in this lesson. Activities stress distinguishing between plurals and possessives.

Lesson Goals
At the conclusion of this lesson, students are expected to:
• identify possessive nouns in sentences;
• write the possessive form of the noun correctly (both singular and plural forms);
• distinguish between possessives and plurals.

Vocabulary
apostrophe	possessive
identify (6)	phrase (6)
ownership (7)	plural (6)
possess (6)	relationship (6)
possession (4)	singular (8)

Teaching Suggestions
1. Discuss the lesson overview and lesson goals.
2. Present the vocabulary and discuss each word.
3. Discuss each answer to each activity.

Follow-Up Activities

1. Have the students write a series of sentences about a trip they have taken, listing the sentences vertically. Have them underline any word that has an apostrophe and circle any word that is a plural noun. Be sure that students are not identifying verb forms that end in -s. Discuss errors with students individually or in small groups. Have the students share their stories in class.

2. Students are likely to have difficulty distinguishing between a singular and plural possessive. To help them with this problem have them make a list of phrases showing nouns in a possessive relationship, such as, *the ship's rudder*. In each case the possessive noun should be singular. Then, have the class offer a matching plural possessive, such as *the ships' rudders*. Point out that if there is more than one ship, there must be more than one rudder. Note: a proper noun cannot be used in this exercise. *Ted's sister* cannot be changed to *Teds' sister*. This drill will be most helpful if done on the chalkboard with the entire group.

Chapter Review

The Chapter Review consists of four exercises that present all of the topics, rules, and concepts included in Chapter 1. Lesson 1 tests the students' ability to identify nouns and to evaluate their ability to recognize proper nouns. Lesson 2 teaches singular and plural nouns. Lesson 3 tests mastery of possessive forms and includes all of the usage rules in the chapter.

Answer Key for Chapter 1
Warm-Up
1. year, Alex, job
2. money, car
3. state, owners, insurance
4. decisions
5. cost, Alex, coverage

Lesson 1, pages 8-16
Activity A
Answers will vary.

Activity B
Answers will vary.

Activity C (only the proper nouns are listed)

3.	Florida	13.	America
5.	Michael J. Fox	15.	John Wayne
6.	China	16.	Christmas
8.	July	17.	Mr. Wilson
9.	Mars	19.	California
10.	England	20.	Wednesday
11.	Benji		

Activity D
1. Utah, Great Salt Lake
2. July
3. *The Sea Wolf*, Jack London
4. Austria, Vienna
5. Babe Ruth

Activity E
1. Houston, Texas
2. River Drive, Apartment 119
3. Robert
4. Northview Senior High
5. Sue
6. North Shore Drive

Activity F
1. Mr. Joe Keller
   Route 2, Box 206
   Marshall, IA 50152

2. Mrs. Karen Thompson
   99 Norris Ave.
   Waterloo, NY 13165

3. Mr. C. J. Simmons
   1580 Eaton Way
   Burke, VA 22015

4. Miss Pam Williams
   41 Maple Ln.
   Lyon, CA 94104

Activity G
1. Alex, South
2. None
3. Baltimore, North Carolina
4. Alex, Tennessee
5. Alex, Florida

Activity H
1. Karl got an A in English.
2. Next year Alex is taking math and social studies.
3. Jennifer signed up for Math 1.
4. Cara enjoys physical education.
5. Danny is going on a field trip in Earth Science 11.

Activity I
1. Wednesday, Alex, Florida
2. Jennifer
3. Alex, Jennifer, South
4. Mr. Jackson
5. Millstream Drive
6. Alex, French
7. None
8. Alex

Activity J
1. team
2. club
3. neighborhood
4. navy
5. jury

Activity K
1. forget-me-not, flower
2. vice-president, graduation
3. Mount McKinley National Park, Alaska
4. Jane, maid-of-honor, wedding
5. Kim, toothbrush, toothpaste, trip

Activity L
1. fever
2. law
3. price
4. emergency
5. hunger
6. excitement
7. year
8. love
9. disaster
10. courage

Lesson Review
1. Alex Jones, car
2. week, amount, money
3. money, bank, interest
4. decision, car
5. car, mileage
6. Alex, ad, newspaper
7. phone number, appointment
8. Alex, automobiles, weeks
9. car, price
10. Alex, feeling, purchase

Lesson 2, pages 17-21
Activity A
1. bunches
2. addresses
3. cars
4. foxes
5. books
6. patches
7. benches
8. schools
9. ladders
10. mountains
11. axes
12. watches
13. teams
14. rivers
15. wishes
16. witches
17. ideas
18. taxes
19. sleds
20. icicles
21. quizzes

Activity B
1. singular
2. plural
3. singular
4. singular
5. singular
6. plural
7. singular
8. singular
9. plural
10. singular
11. plural
12. singular
13. singular
14. plural
15. singular
16. singular
17. plural
18. plural
19. plural
20. plural

Activity C
1. monkeys
2. chimneys
3. countries
4. bodies
5. journeys
6. injuries
7. armies
8. navies
9. bays
10. days

Activity D
1. spies, countries, ladies
2. bodies
3. injuries

Activity E
1. men, deer
2. sheep
3. trout
4. Series
5. loaves, potatoes

Activity F
1. calves
2. beliefs
3. feet
4. men
5. teeth
6. foremen
7. teams
8. knives
9. ladies
10. monkeys
11. tomatoes
12. potatoes
13. mice
14. heroes
15. deer
16. chiefs
17. buses
18. moose
19. chairmen
20. elves
Sentences will vary.

Lesson Review
Part A
1. hours
2. people
3. clothes
4. guests
5. groups
6. snacks

Part B
1. women
2. sheep
3. geese
4. tomatoes
5. lives
6. heroes
7. keys
8. spies
9. children
10. cities
11. taxes
12. policies
13. dishes
14. potatoes
15. addresses
16. deer
17. paths
18. agents
19. parties
20. knives
21. trout
22. mice
23. stereos
24. businesses

Lesson 3, pages 22-26
Activity A
1. Alex's - possessive
2. pages - plural
3. friends - plural
4. friend's - possessive
5. car's - possessive
6. tires - plural

Activity B
1. albums' - plural
2. sofa's - singular
3. television's - singular
4. mice's - plural
5. children's - plural

Activity C
1. chapter's, chapters'
2. job's, jobs'
3. agent's, agents'
4. thing's, things'
5. person's, persons'
6. noun's, nouns'
7. state's, states'
8. goose's, geese's
9. president's, presidents'
10. audience's, audiences'
11. fox's, foxes'
12. wife's, wives'
13. child's, children's
14. man's, men's

15. church's, churches'
16. foot's, feet's
17. crowd's, crowds'
18. sunflower's, sunflowers'
19. navy's, navies'
20. monkey's, monkeys'

Activity D
1. two cents' worth
2. two week's vacation
3. a minute's wait
4. five dollars' worth
5. week's end

Lesson Review
Part A
1. Alex's
2. Mr. Wilson's
3. men's
4. salespersons'
5. Mr. Wilson's

Part B
1. parents - plural
2. world's - possessive
3. Jake's - possessive
4. family's - possessive
5. women's - possessive
6. matches - plural
7. crowds - plural
8. trip's - possessive

Chapter Review
Part A
1. party
2. Jake, Terri, parents, room
3. Mrs. Griffin, living room
4. Records, glasses, bowls
5. Jake, Terri, friends', mess
6. end, evening

Part B
1. August, Terri, Jake
2. Terri, Wilson High School
3. Jake, Hanover Community College
4. Mr. Jackson's
5. Terri, French
6. Jake, English
7. Jake, South
8. English
9. "My First Trip to Florida"

Part C

1. wolves   6. monkeys
2. cities   7. houses
3. quizzes   8. parties
4. teachers   9. children
5. students   10. teeth

Part D

1. Brian
2. Star Wars
3. Wednesday
4. early show

5. English
6. Hanover Community College
7. Basic Computers I
8. computer operator
9. traffic
10. college's
11. team's
12. Jake's
13. Terri's
14. dollar's
15. world's

Chapter 2
The Pronoun

Overview

The activities in Chapter 2 are designed to teach students to recognize pronouns and their antecedents. Each of the five lessons focuses on one kind of pronoun. The kinds of pronouns introduced are: personal, relative, interrogative, demonstrative, and indefinite. The correct usage of pronouns is stressed.

Chapter Goals

At the conclusion of Chapter 2, students are expected to:
- recognize pronouns in sentences;
- identify the various kinds of pronouns;
- recognize correct and incorrect usage of pronouns in sentences.

Teaching Suggestions
1. Discuss the chapter overview.
2. Discuss the chapter goals.
3. Read the introductory material to the students. Do the Warm-Up exercises and discuss the correct answers.

Lesson 1. Personal Pronouns
Overview

Lesson 1 presents the personal pronouns, including the -*self* pronouns. The activities stress identification of personal pronouns and recognition of antecedents.

Lesson Goals

At the conclusion of Lesson 1, students are expected to:
- identify personal pronouns in sentences;
- identify the antecedents of those pronouns.

Vocabulary

antecedent (11)	personal (9)
compound (6)	phrase (6)
distinguish (6)	pronoun
express (4)	refer (6)
feminine (7)	replace (6)
gender (10)	screwdriver (5)
identify (6)	spicy (5)
masculine (7)	subject (5)
neuter (11)	substitute (6)
object (4)	

Teaching Suggestions
1. Use the vocabulary words as part of your instruction. Stress the terms *antecedent*, *gender*, *neuter*, and *personal*, as they may be new to students.
2. Have students memorize the Personal Pronoun Chart on page 33 in the text and reproduce it from memory.
3. Have students do the five activities independently. Discuss the correct responses at the conclusion of each activity.

Follow-Up Activities
1. Select a short passage from a literature text or a magazine. Have the students identify personal pronouns and antecedents.
2. Provide a picture or other stimulus. Have the students write several sentences. Then have them make a list of the pronouns they used and identify the antecedent of each one.

Lesson 2. Relative Pronouns
Overview

In Lesson 2, students are introduced to the relative pronouns, including the compound relative pronouns. Activities stress recognition of the relative pronouns as well as correct usage.

Lesson Goals

At the conclusion of Lesson 2, students are expected to:
- identify relative pronouns in sentences;
- identify the antecedents of those pronouns.

Vocabulary

antique (6)	mink (6)
genuine (6)	pearl (5)
include (5)	prefer (6)
inspect (5)	relative (5)
mechanic (6)	

Teaching Suggestions
1. Explain that the relative pronouns comprise a small group of words that are used frequently in speech and writing. It is important to understand that some relative pronouns refer only

to people, and some refer only to things. One relative pronoun, *that*, can refer to people or things.

2. Activity D helps students distinguish between pronouns and nouns. Activity E aids students in recognizing the difference between personal pronouns and relative pronouns.

Follow-Up Activities
1. Have students make up lists of words that include only nouns or pronouns. Then, they are to identify each word in the lists.
2. Have the students use the list of words in Activity E in original sentences.

Lesson 3. Pronouns That Ask Questions
Overview
The purpose of Lesson 3 is to introduce students to the interrogative pronouns. Each of these pronouns can also be used as a relative pronoun. The activities are designed to help students to recognize situations in which the pronouns *who*, *which*, and *what* are used to ask direct and indirect questions.

Lesson Goals
At the conclusion of Lesson 3, students are expected to:
• locate interrogative, personal, and relative pronouns in sentences;
• identify each kind of pronoun.

Vocabulary
assignment (6)	interrogative
definite (6)	parentheses
indefinite (8)	review (5)
indirect	

Teaching Suggestions
1. Review personal and relative pronouns.
2. Discuss the meanings of these pairs of words:
   definite — indefinite
   direct — indirect
3. Be sure that students understand the meaning of the word interrogative: "asking a question."

Follow-Up Activity
Have each person in the class write a sentence using either *who*, *which*, or *what*. Use the sentences to reinforce the concepts of direct and indirect questions. Read the sentences aloud or write them on the chalkboard. Have the students change them from direct to indirect questions, or vice versa.

Lesson 4. Demonstrative Pronouns
Overview
Lesson 4 introduces and provides practice with demonstrative pronouns. Students identify these parts of speech and determine their correct usage.

Lesson Goals
At the conclusion of Lesson 4, students are expected to:
• identify demonstrative pronouns in sentences;
• distinguish among personal, relative, interrogative, and demonstrative pronouns.

Vocabulary
demonstrative

Teaching Suggestions
1. Present the lesson by reading the information on page 45 orally to the students. Have several student demonstrate the difference between *this* and *that*, and *these* and *those* by giving pairs of sentences.
2. Review the meaning of singular and plural.
3. Prior to conducting the Lesson Review, review the kinds of pronouns presented in previous lessons (personal, relative, and interrogative).

Follow-Up Activities
1. Have several students prepare bulletin board displays illustrating the different kinds of pronouns.
2. Have each student write several sentences using either *this* or *that*, *these* or *those*. Use the sentences to prepare additional drills similar to Activity B on page 46 in the text.

Lesson 5. Indefinite Pronouns
Overview
Lesson 5 introduces the concept of indefinite pronouns. Students practice recognizing these pronouns. They are then introduced to correct usage of verbs and other pronouns in sentences that contain indefinite pronouns.

Lesson Goal
At the end of the lesson, students will identify indefinite pronouns in sentences.

Vocabulary
feminine (7)	neuter (11)
gender (10)	plural (6)
indefinite (8)	previous (6)
masculine (7)	replace (6)
mention (4)	singular (8)

Teaching Suggestions
1. Begin this lesson by presenting the vocabulary words. Write them on the chalkboard and discuss their meanings. Most of the words have been introduced in previous lessons; however, a careful review is advisable.
2. Read the introductory information and do Activity A on page 49 orally with the class. Explain that *is* and *are* are used with singular and plural nouns, respectively. Similarly, *has* and *have* are used with singular and plural nouns.
3. Review the meanings of *gender*, *masculine*, *feminine*, *neuter*, and *antecedent*.

Follow-Up Activity
Find a short selection in a literature book or magazine. Have the students locate the indefinite pronouns.

Chapter Review
Before beginning Part A, go over meanings, examples, and usage for each kind of pronoun introduced in this chapter.

Review Activities
1. Divide the class into five groups. Have each group prepare usage drills for one type of pronoun. Tell the students to provide answers. Use these drills with the entire class.

2. Have each student write several sentences about a topic, including several pronouns in the sentences. Then, have the students make a list of the pronouns used in the sentences. They should identify the kind of pronoun and the antecedent of each one.
3. Have each student in the class make up a sentence. Give each person a particular kind of pronoun to include. Then, have other students identify the kind of pronoun in each sentence. For example:
Teacher: Make up a sentence using a demonstrative pronoun.
Student: That is your desk.
Second Student: The demonstrative pronoun is *that*.
4. Use the Personal Pronoun Chart on page 33 in the text and have each student describe a pronoun in the same manner as Activity A on that page. Have other students identify the pronoun that is described. For example:
Student: What is the first person, plural, nominative pronoun?
Answer: We

Answer Key for Chapter 2
Warm-Up A
1.	her	4.	That
2.	She	5.	us
3.	They	6.	we

Warm-Up B
1. They - Laura and Katie
2. She - Ms. Delente
3. him - James Melcher
4. it - phone number
5. me - Katie

Warm-Up C
1.	I	4.	his
2.	us	5.	himself
3.	Which		

Lesson 1, pages 31-36
Activity A
1.	they	5.	their, theirs
2.	it	6.	me
3.	our, ours	7.	your, yours
4.	you	8.	you

Activity B
1. them
2. They
3. It
4. him
5. Her
6. mine
7. our
8. She
9. We

Activity C
1. They
2. me
3. it
4. Her
5. her
6. she
7. my

Activity D
1. her - Jennifer
2. She - Jennifer
3. They - Jennifer and Michelle
   they - Jennifer and Michelle
4. I - Jennifer
5. You - Jennifer; my - Michelle;
   We - Jennifer and Michelle
6. me - Jennifer

Lesson Review
1. It - day
2. her - Katie
3. She - Katie; herself - Katie
4. She - Katie; her - Katie
5. her - Katie; her - Katie; herself - Katie
6. She - Katie
7. She - Katie; he - James
8. We - Katie and James

Lesson 2, pages 37-40
Activity A
1. that
2. that
3. who
4. which
5. whose

Activity B
1. who - man
2. whom - man
3. which - cars
4. that - car
5. that - screwdriver

Activity C
1. whatever
2. who
3. who
4. whatever
5. that
6. whose
7. Whoever
8. what

Activity D (only pronouns listed)
1. himself
2. whoever
5. which
6. that
7. he
11. I
12. what
13. whom
16. you
17. whatever
18. themselves
19. its
21. she

Activity E

Personal Pronouns	Relative Pronouns
1. we	2. that
5. mine	3. which
6. its	4. what
7. I	9. who
8. you	12. whose
10. ours	15. whom
11. them	16. whichever
13. us	17. that
14. itself	19. whoever
18. themselves	20. whatever
21. he	

Activity F
1. that
2. which
3. whom
4. that

Lesson Review
1. who - mechanic
2. Whoever - Andy or Frank
3. whichever - shoes
4. that - man
5. whichever - steak or chicken
6. whose - friend
7. that - hat
8. that - coat
9. what - the gift (implied antecedent)
10. who - Shamus

Lesson 3, pages 41-44
Activity A
1. Which
2. What
3. who
4. what
5. Who

Activity B
1. Which
2. What
3. Who
4. What
5. whom
6. Who
7. What

Activity C
Interrogative Pronouns Relative Pronouns
3. What
5. which
6. Who
7. Which
8. What
1. whose
2. that
4. whichever
4. that
9. whatever

Lesson Review
1. It - personal
   what - interrogative
   they - personal
2. What - interrogative
3. Whatever - relative
   me - personal
4. Whom - interrogative
   we - personal
   us - personal
5. I - personal
   that - relative
   I - personal
6. which - relative
   he - personal
7. What - interrogative
   it - personal
   I - personal
   that - relative
   I - personal
   her - personal
8. whatever - relative
   you - personal

Lesson 4, pages 45-46
Activity A
1. that
2. Those
3. these
4. that
5. This
6. Those
7. These

Activity B
1. that
2. This
3. Those
4. Those
5. this

Lesson Review
1. which - relative
2. Which - interrogative
   I - personal
   this - demonstrative
   he - personal
3. Whichever - relative
   that - relative
   you - personal
   his - personal
4. that - relative
   he - personal
5. What - interrogative
   I - personal
6. them - personal
7. those - demonstrative
   who - relative
   what - interrogative (indirect question)
   he - personal
8. He - personal
   whose - relative

Lesson 5, pages 47-50
Activity A
1. Everyone
2. anyone
3. None
4. one another
5. Few
6. Everyone
7. Every one
8. no one
9. some
10. Everything
11. each other
12. Some
13. nothing
14. someone
15. Other

Activity B
1. is
2. is
3. are
4. is
5. has
6. his
7. her
8. their
9. his
10. its

Activity C
Answers will vary.

Lesson Review

1. Everyone
2. All
3. Everybody
4. Nobody, anything
5. someone
6. all, someone
7. No one, anything

Chapter Review
Part A

1. It - personal
2. Everyone - indefinite
   his - personal
3. No one - indefinite
4. Everybody - indefinite
   his - personal
   her - personal
5. Who - interrogative
6. That - demonstrative
7. She - personal
   everything - indefinite
8. I - personal
   my - personal
9. They - personal
   what - relative

Part B

1. himself
2. Which (choice)
3. Which (choice)
4. that (*what* cannot refer to a person)
5. is (*Nobody* is singular)
6. these (objects close at hand)
7. ourselves
8. We (subject)
9. its (no apostrophe in possessive pronouns)
10. whatever (no choice between specific objects implied)
11. themselves
12. this (stereo is close at hand)

Chapter 3
The Adjective

Overview

Chapter 3 is divided into six lessons. Lesson 1 introduces the adjective and stresses the identification of the noun or pronoun that the adjective is describing. The other five lessons focus on different types of adjectives, degrees of comparison, and usage rules.

Chapter Goals

At the conclusion of Chapter 3, the students are expected to:
- locate adjectives in sentences;
- identify the noun or pronoun that the adjective is describing.

Teaching Suggestions

1. Read the introductory material with the class. The adjective is defined. Placement of the adjective in sentences is explained. In Warm-Up A, students are not expected to identify the articles as adjectives.
2. You may have students complete the three Warm-Up exercises independently and use the results as a diagnostic tool. You may also do all three activities orally with the class. In either case, discuss the correct answers.

Follow-Up Activity

Prepare a bulletin board display that illustrates adjectives, such as a mural depicting school activities. On separate cards, print adjectives that describe the people, places, things, or events in the mural. Attach the cards to the mural.

Lesson 1. What Is an Adjective?
Overview

In Lesson 1 students are introduced to the definitions of several kinds of adjectives. Activities focus on two basic skills: locating adjectives in sentences and identifying the noun or pronoun that each adjective describes.

Lesson Goals

At the conclusion of the lesson, students are expected to:
- locate adjectives in sentences;
- identify the noun or pronoun that the adjective is describing.

Vocabulary

adjective	equipment (5)
characteristic (6)	limit (5)
chilly (5)	possessive
college (5)	quantity (6)
cucumber	reel (5)
define (7)	rod (5)
demonstrative	shimmer (5)
describe (5)	splendid (5)
elect (5)	away (5)
emphasis (8)	wondrous (6)

Teaching Suggestions

1. Discuss the definition of an adjective and the various types of adjectives given on pages 55-56. Have students identify the noun or pronoun that each adjective describes.
2. Do Activity A on page 56. When reviewing the correct answers, have students identify the noun or pronoun that each adjective describes.
3. Have students share their responses to Activities D and E with the class.

Follow-Up Activity

Find a short selection in a literature book, newspaper, or magazine. Have students locate all of the adjectives and identify the noun or pronoun each adjective describes. This activity will help students relate the lesson to the material they read. It will also increase their awareness in written material.

Lesson 2. The Articles — A, An, The
Overview

Lesson 2 reinforces the concept that articles are adjectives. Activities are designed to foster correct usage of articles in sentences.

Lesson Goals

At the conclusion of Lesson 2, students are expected to:
- distinguish between situations in which the articles *a* and *an* are correct;
- recognize that the article that precedes a plural noun is the article *the*.

Vocabulary

argument (6)	indefinite (8)
assignment (6)	plural (6)
definite (3)	singular (8)
hostile (7)	

Teaching Suggestions
1. Discuss the information and definitions on page 59.
2. Be sure students can pronounce and give the meanings of the vocabulary words.
3. Review vowels and consonants. Stress that the article *an* is used before a vowel sound, not just a vowel letter. Also, stress that the article is governed by the word immediately following it rather than the noun it describes, such as ***an** open door*.

Follow-Up Activity
Have students prepare additional sentences similar to those used in Activity B on page 60. Use these sentences in additional drills, dividing the class into two teams. The objective of the game is to try to stump the other team. A correct answer receives one point. Alternate sentences between the teams. The first team to obtain a score of 15 wins.

Lesson 3. Adjectives That Are Capitalized
Overview
The activities in this lesson provide practice with proper adjectives.

Lesson Goal
Students are expected to locate proper adjectives in sentences and to capitalize the first letter of these words.

Vocabulary

career (6)	political (6)
commercial (6)	prefer (6)
education (5)	proper (5)
literature (6)	

Teaching Suggestions
1. Review or teach the meanings of any vocabulary words that are unfamiliar to students.

2. Review the topic of proper nouns (chapter 1). A proper adjective is either a proper noun used as an adjective or the adjective form of the noun.
3. Activities in Lesson 3 are suitable for independent work followed by a discussion of the correct responses.

Follow-Up Activities
1. Explain that nouns are sometimes changed to adjectives by adding certain suffixes. Examples are: German — Germanic; America — American; Italy — Italian; Swede — Swedish. Provide students with a list of countries, cities, and nationalities. Have them check the dictionary to find the adjective forms of these words.
2. Point out that some proper nouns do not add suffixes and can be used either as proper nouns or proper adjectives, depending on their uses in sentences. Have students prepare additional lists of such words and use them in sentences, one sentence as a noun, another as an adjective.
For example:
Idaho is a western state. (noun)
We bought *Idaho* potatoes. (adjective)

Lesson 4. Numbers Used as Adjectives
Overview
The activities in Lesson 4 are designed to focus the students' attention on numbers, both definite and indefinite, which are used to describe nouns and pronouns in sentences. Students must continue to distinguish between pronouns and adjectives in sentences.

Lesson Goals
At the conclusion of Lesson 4, students are expected to:
• locate adjectives in sentences;
• identify the noun or pronoun that each adjective describes.

Vocabulary
exact (6)
indefinite (8)

Teaching Suggestions
1. Review the meanings of the words *definite* and *indefinite*. Discuss the definitions, explanations, and examples on page 65.
2. Have students look up the words *few* and *several* in a dictionary and discuss the differences in their meanings.
3. Point out that in the phrase, *all of the students,* the word *of* follows the indefinite pronoun. *All* is not describing students. Contrast that example with the phrase, *all students.* In the second phrase, *all* precedes the noun and describes it. The distinction will become clearer in Chapter 7, which deals with prepositions and prepositional phrases.

Follow-Up Activity
Put the students' sentences from Activity A on the chalkboard or use an overhead projector and a transparency. Have students locate numbers and identify the noun or pronoun each number describes.

Lesson 5. Possessives and Demonstratives Used as Adjectives
Overview
In this lesson, students are made aware of nouns and pronouns that are used as adjectives in sentences. Students also learn the distinction between a demonstrative pronoun used as a pronoun and a demonstrative pronoun used as an adjective.

Lesson Goals
At the conclusion of Lesson 5, students are expected to:
- locate possessives used as adjectives in sentences;
- identify the noun or pronoun that each describes;
- locate demonstratives used as adjectives in sentences.

Vocabulary

demonstrative	raid (5)
possess (4)	solution (6)
possession (6)	suggestion (5)
possessive	

Teaching Suggestions
1. Discuss the meanings of the words *possess, possession,* and *possessive.* A word that shows possession (or is possessive) depicts an ownership or relationship.
2. Review the other vocabulary words.
3. Be sure students can distinguish between nouns, pronouns, and adjectives used in sentences.
4. Point out that a possessive pronoun used as an adjective in a sentence can describe a possessive noun in that sentence. That possessive noun can then describe another noun. Example: *my father's* birthday
5. Show that a possessive noun can also describe a noun, which in turn describes a third noun. Example: *Jack's father's* car
6. Be sure that students can pronounce and spell the term *demonstrative.* They should be able to identify all four demonstrative pronouns.
7. Activities may be completed orally or independently. Review the correct answers.

Follow-Up Activity
Using a short selection from literature, a newspaper, or a magazine, have students locate possessive nouns and pronouns used as adjectives; and also locate demonstrative adjectives and pronouns. Be sure they do not confuse the demonstrative that with the relative pronoun *that.*

Lesson 6. Using Adjectives to Make Comparisons
Overview
In this lesson, students learn to identify and write the positive, comparative, and superlative degrees of adjectives. Correct usage is stressed.

Lesson Goal
Students are expected to identify the degree of comparison of adjectives used in sentences.

Vocabulary

athlete (6)	irregular (7)
comparative	positive (6)
compare (5)	superlative (10)
comparison (6)	tennis (5)
consonant	vicious (5)
generous (5)	vowel (5)

Teaching Suggestions

1. Discuss the meaning of the word *compare*. Making comparisons is an abstract activity and can be very difficult for students.

   Point out that an adjective often names some characteristic or quality of the person, place, thing, or idea that it describes. The object being described has that characteristic or quality in a greater or lesser amount, or degree, than other objects.

   Continue the discussion with an example, such as, "Every student in the room has a desk." Are some desks larger than others? smaller? better or worse in some way? Which is the largest? smallest? best or worse? Have students find other examples. Avoid any personal characteristics, such as height, weight, and attractiveness.

2. Give the students a list of adjectives. Have them divide the words into syllables and count the number of syllables.

3. The activities in Lesson 6 will be most effective if they are conducted as oral drills and discussed thoroughly. Be sure that students can pronounce and spell the terms *positive*, *comparative*, and *superlative*.

Follow-Up Activities

1. Explain that a few adjectives cannot be compared. These adjectives are called *absolute superlatives*. The adjective *perfect* is an example. If a student's work is perfect, it is absolutely correct. Another student's work cannot be more perfect or most perfect. Here are some other examples that you can list on the chalkboard for discussion:

honest	correct
everlasting	matchless
vertical	infinite
daily	single
endless	dead
chief	square
round	empty
right	unique

2. Have students use the adjectives in Activities A and C in sentences as either comparatives or superlatives. Use the sentences in a drill. Have the students identify both the adjective and the degree of comparison in each.

Chapter Review
Review Activities

1. Do the Chapter Review on page 76.
2. Have students write several sentences about a topic, using as many adjectives as possible. Have students volunteer to write their sentences on the chalkboard. Then, their classmates should locate the adjectives in each sentence. Here are some suggested topics:
   - Describe a party you gave or attended;
   - Describe the most interesting person you have ever known;
   - Describe your ideal vacation;
   - Describe the city in which you would like to live.

Answer Key for Chapter 3
Warm-Up A

1. autumn, cool, clear   3. long
2. happy, beautiful   4. wondrous, splendid

Warm-Up B

1. Sharon's - homeroom   4. good - president
2. new - officers   5. close - election
   school - year
3. smart - Sharon
   loyal - Sharon
   fun - Sharon

Warm-Up C

1. history - adjective   4. meeting - noun
2. history - noun   5. south - adjective
3. meeting - adjective   6. south - noun

Lesson 1, pages 55-58
Activity A

1. part-time, Mr. Jackson's
2. sporting, men's
3. many, different
4. His, favorite, fishing
5. Those, new, expensive
6. my

Activity B

1. expensive - reel   4. sure - I
   new - reel   several - fish
2. fishing - trip   big - fish
   his - friends   5. next - morning

3. This - reel   6. hopeful - They
   great - reel

Activity C
1. beautiful - lake   4. eight - hours
   that - morning   5. late - afternoon
2. large - fish   many - fish
3. his - rod and reel   6. tired - They
   trusty - rod and reel   happy - They
   old - rod and reel

Activity D
Answers will vary.

Activity E
Answers will vary.

Lesson Review
1. chilly - weather   4. David's - class
2. his - coat   favorite - class
   winter - coat   5. easy - Math
3. several - classes   6. his - car

Lesson 2, pages 59-61
Activity A
There are sixteen articles in the sentences.

Activity B
1. an   6. an
2. an   7. an
3. a   8. an
4. an   9. a
5. an   10. an

Activity C
1. the (a certain coat)
2. the (plural noun)
3. the (plural noun)
4. the
5. an
6. the

Lesson Review
1. a   6. a (consonant sound)
2. the (plural noun)   7. the (plural noun)
3. an (vowel sound)   8. a (consonant sound)
4. an (vowel sound)   9. an (vowel sound)
5. an (vowel sound)   10. the

Lesson 3, pages 62-64
Activity A
1. none   5. none
2. French   6. Indian
3. English, Shakespearean 7. Wednesday-only
4. American

Activity B
Answers will vary.

Activity C
Answers will vary.

Activity D
1. French - adjective   6. French - adjective
2. Philadelphia - noun 7. Spain - noun
3. Philadelphia - adjective 8. Spanish - noun
4. Frank - noun   9. Spanish - adjective
5. Irish - adjective   10. Chevrolet - adjective

Lesson Review
1. German   4. American
2. Ford   5. Swiss
3. Swiss   6. Spanish

Lesson 4, pages 65-67
Activity A
Answers will vary.

Activity B
1. Twenty-five - people 4. Several - members
2. One - student   5. Most - students
3. few - weeks

Activity C
1. eighty - adjective   6. Most - adjective
2. several - adjective 7. six - adjective
3. Everyone - pronoun   8. No one - pronoun
4. Many - adjective   9. Some - adjective
5. few - adjective   10. Others - pronoun

Lesson Review
1. several - friends   5. three - hot dogs
   City - zoo   some - lemonade
2. three - chimpanzees 6. All - birds
3. eight - lions   7. several - hour
   six - tigers   8. Few - people
4. many - monkeys

Lesson 5, pages 68-71
Activity A
1. my - money's*
   money's - worth
2. Mr. Jackson's - store
3. His - store
   my - house
4. men's - department
5. my - father's*
   father's - birthday
6. His - birthday
7. our - fun
   year's - presents
8. Dad's - face

*A possessive noun may be described by another adjective.

Activity B
1. Jack's - bike
2. His - coat
3. My - mother's
   mother's - ring
4. my - garden
5. Whose - pencil

Activity C
1. This - adjective
2. that - adjective
   this - adjective
3. those - adjective
4. that - adjective
5. This - pronoun
6. That - pronoun

Activity D
1. that - day
2. those - snacks
3. that - cupboard
4. those - things
5. These - potato chips

Lesson Review
1. their - homework
2. Vince's - answer
3. your - answer
4. his - answer
5. Vince's - face
6. my - answer
7. our - work
8. Vince's - suggestion
9. your - mother's;
   mother's - dessert
10. David's - refrigerator

Lesson 6, pages 72-75
Activity A
1. younger, youngest
2. older, oldest
3. kinder, kindest
4. shorter, shortest
5. greener, greenest
6. slower, slowest
7. later, latest*
8. stricter, strictest
9. brighter, brightest
10. nicer, nicest*

*If the adjective ends in an -e, add only -r or -st.

Activity B
1. least comfortable - superlative
2. terrible - positive
3. most talented - superlative
4. sadder - comparative
5. less expensive - comparative

Activity C
Answers will vary.

Activity D
1. reddest
2. taller
3. thinner
4. oldest
5. more comfortable
6. best
7. easier
8. least generous
9. more successful

Lesson Review
1. comparative
2. positive; comparative
3. positive
4. comparative
5. superlative
6. comparative
7. positive; comparative
8. comparative

Chapter Review
1. a - party
   Halloween - party
2. The - party
   a - evening
   Saturday - evening
3. David's - parents
   their - permission
4. the - living room
   orange - streamers
   black - streamers
5. the - skeletons
   horrible - skeletons
   the - witches
   ugliest - witches
   the - store
6. some - decorations
   old - decorations
   the - attic
7. fifty - apples
   red - apples
   ten - gallons
8. an - pumpkin
   enormous - pumpkin
9. Several - people
   more - food
10. the - party
    the - one
    best - one

Chapter 4
The Action Verb

Overview

Chapter 4 consists of seven lessons designed to develop the concept of the verb as a word that expresses action. The state-of-being verbs are introduced in Chapter 5. Students first practice locating verbs in sentences. Lesson 3 presents verb tenses. Lessons 4, 5, and 6 present the progressive forms, emphatic forms, and conditional forms. Lesson 7 explains active and passive verbs.

Chapter Goals

At the conclusion of Chapter 4, students are expected to:
• locate verbs and verb phrases in sentences;
• recognize correct verb form.

Vocabulary
thud (5)

Teaching Suggestions
1. Discuss the examples and introductory information. Tell students that state-of-being verbs will be presented in the next chapter.
2. Discuss the chapter goals so that the students are aware of them.
3. Have students complete the Warm-Up exercises on page 78. Discuss the correct answers.

Lesson 1. Finding the Verb in a Sentence
Overview

The purpose of Lesson 1 is to develop the concept of the verb as the word in a sentence that expresses the action. The students are directed to ask who or what is doing something (subject) and what the subject is doing (verb).

Lesson Goal

Students are expected to identify the verb or verb phrase in a sentence.

Vocabulary

computer (8)	process (6)
doughnut (5)	schedule (6)
employee (6)	secretary (5)
haul (5)	solution (6)

Teaching Suggestions
1. Discuss the definitions of the vocabulary words. None of these words relate to the concepts being taught.
2. The word *action* should be familiar to the students; however, a discussion of its meaning would be useful. Explain that there can be mental as well as physical actions and that action does not necessarily involve visible movement. Have students suggest a list of words that express action. Write the list on the chalkboard.
3. After each activity, discuss the correct answers.

Follow-Up Activity

Have students write several sentences about a recent school, local, or national event. Tell them that every sentence must include an action verb. The subject must be doing something in the sentence. Tell students that the main verb cannot be *is*, *are*, *was*, or *were*, but these words may be used as helping verbs.

Lesson 2. Transitive and Intransitive Verbs
Overview

Lesson 2 introduces the student to transitive and intransitive verbs. Direct objects are also discussed.

Lesson Goal

At the conclusion of Lesson 2, students should be able to distinguish between transitive and intransitive verbs.

Vocabulary
intransitive
transitive
motorcycle

Teaching Suggestions
1. Explain the difference between a transitive and an intransitive verb. Some actions cannot be performed without another person or thing to receive the action. The action is trans-

ferred to the other person or thing. For example, Andy bought is not a complete idea. If someone said those words, we would wonder *bought what?* The action is transitive. It cannot be completed without another thing. The action must be transferred to something. The action expressed by an intransitive verb, however, can be done by a person or thing by itself. We can *walk*, or *sing*, or *laugh* without another person or thing to receive the action.

2. Conduct the Warm-Up activities with the class and discuss all answers.

Follow-Up Activity

If the students continue to have difficulty with the concept of intransitive and transitive verbs, have them act out verbs such as, hit*, read*, paint*, choose*, leave*, laugh, walk, skip, jump, give*, and kneel. The transitive verbs are marked with an asterisk. The students will need to use another person or object to complete the action. If the verb is intransitive, they will be able to do the action without the involvement of an additional person or object.

Lesson 3. Verbs Also Express Tense
Overview

Lesson 3 introduces students to the three simple tenses — present, past, future — and the three perfect tenses — present perfect, past perfect, and future perfect.

Students also learn the subject-verb agreement rule regarding the third person singular and plural subjects. They are encouraged to memorize the parts of the irregular verb *to have*. Other commonly used irregular verbs are also presented.

Lesson Goals

At the conclusion of Lesson 3, students are expected to:
• find the verb or verb phrase in sentences;
• identify the tense of each verb.

Vocabulary

compound (6)	past participle
infinitive	separate (5)
irregular	tackle (6)
opponent (7)	tense (6)

Teaching Suggestions

1. Students will encounter the words *opponent* and *tackle* in the lesson activities. Be sure they are familiar with these words.
2. Discuss the term *tense*. Students should know that a verb expresses action and also expresses tense, or time. Point out that *-ed* is a suffix that means past time. The helping verbs *will* or *shall* usually indicate future time.
   Note that *will* and *shall* can also be used as conditional helping verbs (see Lesson 6). The meaning is different; but because the forms of the verbs are identical, students are not likely to make usage errors. For example:
   Future: I *will* go tomorrow.
   Conditional: The basket *will* hold 25 oranges.
3. Tell students that endings and helping verbs are used to express different tenses. The root word is the infinitive; the infinitive is the same as the present tense in all cases except for the verb *to be*.
4. Review the meanings of *regular* and *irregular*, *singular* and *plural*.
5. Discuss the correct answers to the activities.
6. A list of some commonly used irregular verbs is presented on page 91. Students must recognize that the past and past participle forms of regular verbs are the same and both end in *-ed*. With irregular verbs, the past and past participle forms may be different. Neither verb form ends in *-ed*. Students should memorize these verb forms.

Follow-Up Activities

1. Have students use the verbs from the list on page 91 to write sentences using verbs in all six tenses, as they did in Activity H.
2. Have students write a news story about a recent school, local, or national event. Instruct them to use only action verbs. A model is given as the Lesson Review on page 93.

Lesson 4. The Progressive Forms
Overview

Lesson 4 presents the progressive forms. Students must learn the forms of the verb *to be*. They must also distinguish between the regular tenses and the progressive verb forms.

Lesson Goals

At the conclusion of Lesson 4, students are expected to:

- write the twelve forms of a regular verb;
- use them correctly in sentences;
- locate the verb or verb phrase in a sentence and identify the tense.

Vocabulary

accompany (5)   popularity
orphanage (6)   progressive (7)
popular (4)

Teaching Suggestions

1. Discuss the term progressive. Explain that verb forms that end in *-ing* and use *to be* as a helping verb express action, tense, and the idea that the action is ongoing (continuing). Put several examples on the chalkboard to help students understand the difference in meaning between the regular and progressive forms.

    For example:

    He *works* at the store every day.

    He *is working* there now.

2. Have students produce from memory the chart showing the forms of *to be* on page 95.

3. Explain that verbs have two kinds of participles: present and past. The past participle is used with the perfect tenses (with *have* as a helper). The present participle is used to form the progressive forms (with *be* as a helper). The past participle usually ends in *-ed*; the present participle always ends in *-ing*. A verb can express perfect tense and progressive tense at the same time; therefore, both *have* and *be* are used as helping verbs.

    For example:

    He *has been* practicing.

Follow-Up Activities

1. Provide an additional drill by assigning exercises as described in Activities C and D on page 96.

2. Have students use assigned verbs in sentences. All twelve forms should be presented as described in the first part of the Lesson Review on page 98.

Lesson 5. The Emphatic Form — The Verb with *Do* or *Did*

Overview

Lesson 5 presents the verb *to do* as a helping verb in the emphatic form. *To do* is also presented as the main verb in a sentence. Students should distinguish *to do* as a helping verb from the verb used as a main verb.

Lesson Goals

At the conclusion of Lesson 5, students are expected to:

- identify verbs or verb phrases in sentences. Each verb will include the verb *to do* either as a main or helping verb;
- identify the tense of each verb or verb phrase.

Vocabulary

emphasize (7)   emphatic (11)   negative (8)

Teaching Suggestions

1. Point out that the verbs, *have*, *be*, and *do* may be used as helping verbs and main verbs.

2. Discuss the terms *emphatic* and *emphasize*. Be sure that students can pronounce and spell each word correctly. Some synonyms for the adjective emphatic are: forceful, stressed, powerful, and conspicuous. The verb form is *emphasize*.

3. The negative words used in the lesson are *not* and *never*. *Do* as a helping verb emphasizes the negative word.

    Example: He *went* home.

    He *did not* go home.

4. Explain that *to do* as a main verb means to perform some action. The verb is always followed by a noun that names the action.

    I *did* my homework.

    I *do* the dishes.

    Explain that *do* can be a helping verb for itself.

    I *did* not *do* my homework.

    Do you *do* exercises every day?

    Point out that only *do* and *did* are used as helping verbs. The main verb will always be in the present or infinitive form.

    Present: I *do* not *like* lima beans.

    Past: I *did* not like lima beans.

    Done (the past participle) is not used as a helping verb.

Follow-Up Activities

1. Provide students with a list of verbs in the present (infinitive) form. Have students use these verbs in sentences using *do* (*did*) first as a question, and then to emphasize a negative word.

2. Have students write ten original sentences, using *do* as a main verb in five sentences and as a helping verb in five sentences. Have students read their work to the class. Other students can identify the verb and tell whether *do* is used as a helping or main verb or both.

Lesson 6. The Conditional Forms
Overview

Lesson 6 introduces the helping verbs that are used in the conditional forms. These verbs are used only as helping verbs, never as main verbs.

Lesson Goal

At the conclusion of Lesson 6, students are expected to identify verb phrases that express the conditional form.

Vocabulary

combine (6)	purse (5)
compound (6)	requirement (8)
condition (4)	responsibility (6)
conditional (8)	

Teaching Suggestions

1. Read the introductory information and examples. Discuss the meanings of each helping verb. The technical term for these verbs is *modal*. In some sentences, the main verb is not stated, but it is always understood.

    Did you make your bed?
    No, but I should (make my bed).
    I *would* (make my bed) if I had time.

2. Point out the difference between *will* and *shall* as future indicators and *will* and *shall* as they indicate conditions.

    You *shall* leave.
    (*Shall* expresses an obligation to leave.)
    May I have an apple? Yes, that *will* be fine.
    (*Will* expresses permission or consent.)

3. Explain that *might* is the past form of the verb *may*; however, in current usage, *may* and *might* are used to express different conditions not different tenses.

    May I have an apple?
    Yes, you *may* have one. (permission)
    Are you leaving now?
    I *may* (leave now). (possibility)
    Will you go to Florida?
    I *might* go. (possibility)
    Can you sing? (Do you have the ability?)
    I *could* sing.
    (The ability was there, or you would sing under certain conditions.)
    The basket *will hold* a dozen oranges.
    (It is big enough.)
    The girl *would* do her homework.
    (under certain conditions)
    Would is usually followed by *if...* or *but*.
    He *would like* that movie. (if he saw it)

4. Explain that *must* implies an obligation or responsibility to perform some action.

5. Point out that the helping verbs studied in this lesson can be used with the perfect tense and the progressive and emphatic forms.

Follow-Up Activity

Have students look up each of the conditional helping verbs in a dictionary, write the meanings, then, use the words in sentences.

Lesson 7. Active and Passive Verbs
Overview

In Lesson 7, the concepts of active and passive voice are presented, though the term *voice* is not used in the text. Students recognize verb phrases that are passive and distinguish the passive verb from the progressive form.

Lesson Goal

At the conclusion of Lesson 7, students are expected to identify passive verb phrases in selected sentences.

Vocabulary

defeat (5)	participle
passive (10)	successful (5)

Teaching Suggestions

1. Discuss the meaning of the word *passive*. Passive means to be acted upon without acting in return; taking no part; inactive. A verb is passive when the subject is not doing the action; the subject is acted upon. Therefore, it is actually the subject of the sentence that is passive. The verb changes to agree with the passive subject. For example:

    Active: *Lightning* struck the tree.

    Passive: The tree was struck by *lightning*.

    The verb continues to express action and tense.

2. Point out that the helping verb to be is used to express the progressive form with the present participle (verb form ending in *-ing*). *To be* is used with the past participle to express the passive verb form.

3. Only transitive verbs can be active and passive. A transitive verb is one that has an object. Point out that not every verb can be made passive.

Follow-Up Activity

Have students write two sentences using the verbs listed below, changing the active verb to a passive verb in the second sentence.

For example: I covered my book.

The book was covered by me.

advise	throw	dislike
alarm	like	change
fix	do	wash

Chapter Review

Prior to assigning the Chapter Review, review the concepts and vocabulary presented throughout the chapter. Also, discuss the following vocabulary words:

consecutive (9)	minor (6)
contract (6)	nickname (5)
elect (5)	testify (7)

Review Activities

1. Find a passage in a magazine or newspaper that contains mostly simple or compound (rather than complex) sentences. Have students read each sentence orally and identify the verb/verb phrase. Students should recognize that to be used as a main verb is not an action verb. Tell them that they will study state-of-being verbs in the next chapter.

2. Review the irregular verbs on page 91 and the subject-verb agreement rule. Have students write a sentence using each irregular verb in the past tense, then, in a perfect tense.

3. Have students write several sentences about a person they admire. Have them tell only about specific things the person has done. Each sentence must include an action verb. Have them underline the verb/verb phrase and identify the tense. Students should share their sentences with the class. Other students can identify the verb and the tense in each sentence.

Answer Key for Chapter 4
Warm-Up A

1. brought		6. poured
2. heard		7. sat
3. opened		8. read
4. got		9. turned
5. carried		10. started

Warm-Up B

1. has left		4. are going
2. is driving		5. is thinking
3. is rushing		

Lesson 1, pages 79-82
Activity A

1. parked		4. went
2. greeted		5. started
3. walked		

Activity B

	Subject	Verb
1.	everyone	worked
2.	people	sorted
3.	Others	loaded
4.	trucks	hauled
5.	carriers	deliver
6.	mail	goes
7.	Mr. Jones	works
8.	He	prepares
9.	He	gives
10.	computer	prints

Activity C

1. parked, entered
2. drank, ate
3. read
4. scheduled
5. rang
6. picked*, said
7. talked, hung*
8. returned

*Picked up and hung up are acceptable answers.

Activity D

1. had
2. thought
3. have
4. wondered
5. decided
6. knew

Activity E

Answers will vary.

Lesson Review

1. work
2. stream
3. collect
4. comes
5. bring
6. unload
7. sort
8. put
9. deliver
10. processes

Lesson 2, pages 83-84

Activity A

1. money
2. cards
3. contest
4. place
5. solo

It is not incorrect to include the adjectives in your answers.

Activity B

1. transitive
2. intransitive
3. transitive
4. intransitive
5. intransitive
6. transitive

Lesson Review

1. transitive
2. intransitive
3. transitive
4. transitive
5. transitive

Lesson 3, pages 85-93

Activity A

1. will play - future
2. practices - present
3. wondered - past
4. called - past
5. talked - past
6. believe - present
7. knows - present
8. want - present

Activity B

1. hopes
2. plays
3. goes
4. play
5. decides
6. looks
7. works

Activity C

1. have
2. has
3. had
4. have
5. have

Activity D

1. helping verb
2. helping verb
3. main verb
4. main verb
5. main verb

Activity E

1. has acted, had acted, will have acted
2. has discussed, had discussed, will have discussed
3. has improved, had improved, will have improved
4. has locked, had locked, will have locked
5. has moved, had moved, will have moved
6. has offered, had offered, will have offered
7. has opened, had opened, will have opened
8. has passed, had passed, will have passed
9. has snarled, had snarled, will have snarled
10. has whispered, had whispered, will have whispered

Activity F

1. walks, walked, will walk, has walked, had walked, will have walked
2. works, worked, will work, has worked, had worked, will have worked
3. fishes, fished, will fish, has fished, had fished, will have fished
4. drives, drove, will drive, has driven, had driven, will have driven
5. roars, roared, will roar, has roared, had roared, will have roared

Activity G

1. played
2. applied
3. buys
4. played
5. enjoyed
6. hurried
7. replied
8. stayed
9. terrifies
10. testified

Activity H
1. taught
2. gave
3. saw
4. eaten
5. seen
6. begun
7. knew or knows
8. caught
9. came or comes
10. gone
11. went or goes
12. chosen

Activity I
1. has given
2. has rung
3. Have heard
4. has seen
5. have seen
6. Have studied
7. will bring
8. have gone
9. had had
10. had enjoyed

Activity J
1. future
2. past
3. present
4. past
5. future
6. past
7. past perfect
8. present perfect
9. future
10. future perfect

Lesson Review
1. enjoyed - past
2. threw - past
3. ended - past
4. made - past
5. had tackled - past perfect
6. fumbled - past
7. recovered - past
8. marched - past
9. scored - past
10. will have extended - future perfect
11. offer - present
12. came - past
13. will face - future
14. hopes - present
15. have looked - present perfect

Lesson 4, pages 94-98
Activity A
1. is practicing
2. was practicing
3. will be practicing
4. has been practicing
5. has been practicing
6. will have been practicing

Activity B
1. been
2. be
3. been
4. been
5. is

Activity C
Answers will vary.

Activity D
1. had gone - past perfect
2. is flying - present progressive
3. will be leaving - future progressive
4. has been packing - present perfect progressive
5. called - past
6. are going - present progressive

Activity E
1. playing
2. played
3. going
4. accompanying
5. raising
6. raised
7. selling
8. sold
9. bought
10. addressing

Lesson Review
Part A
1. sharpens
2. sharpened
3. will sharpen
4. has (have) sharpened
5. had sharpened
6. will have sharpened
7. is (am, are) sharpening
8. was (were) sharpening
9. will be sharpening
10. have (has) been sharpening
11. had been sharpening
12. will have been sharpening
Sentences will vary.

Part B
1. played - past
2. earned - past
3. was living - past progressive
4. studied - past
5. had been playing - past perfect progressive
6. joined - past
7. moved - past
8. was playing - past progressive
9. invented - past
10. was recording - past progressive
11. had formed - past perfect
12. loved - past
13. was starring - past progressive
14. continued - past

15. sold - past
16. died - past
17. will remember - future

Lesson 5, pages 99-101
Activity A
1. Did see
2. did find
3. is doing
4. Do read
5. do do

Activity B
1. main verb
2. main verb
3. main verb
4. helping verb
5. main verb
6. helping verb
7. helping verb
8. main verb

Lesson Review
1. do - present
2. Did rake - past
3. have raked - present perfect
4. Does plant - present
5. will have done - future perfect
6. have done - present perfect
7. Did do - past
8. are doing - present progressive
9. did trim - past
10. Did find - past

Lesson 6, pages 102-104
Activity A
1. may stay
2. can play
3. will hold
4. should do
5. must finish

Activity B
1. exercises
2. exercise
3. might
4. go

Activity C
1. will hold
2. should clean
3. must clean
4. can find
5. should have bought
6. might be buying
7. Should buy

Lesson Review
1. might be going
2. could have gone
3. must go
4. would like
5. should pack
6. must take
7. can go
8. may take
9. Should take
10. might rain

Lesson 7, pages 105-106
Activity A
1. active
2. passive
3. active
4. passive
5. passive
6. active

Activity B
Answers will vary.

Activity C
1. was discovered
2. were disturbed
3. was answered
4. was hit
5. was greased

Lesson Review
1. was invented
2. are removed
3. was explored
4. was elected
5. was written
6. was made
7. was settled
8. was killed
9. was defeated
10. was chosen

Chapter Review
Part A
1. began
2. gave
3. played
4. sold
5. pitched, batted
6. won
7. broke
8. had been looking
9. was sent
10. would play
11. continued
12. was hitting
13. would set
14. had hit
15. hit
16. was elected

Part B
1. went
2. play
3. practices
4. want
5. likes
6. has
7. scored
8. hurried
9. testified
10. begun
11. brings
12. knew
13. does
14. is
15. are
16. is
17. finish
18. go
19. must
20. could
21. written
22. baked
23. invented
24. were
25. made

Chapter 5
The State-of-Being Verb

Overview
The activities in Chapter 5 are designed to develop the concept of state-of-being, to help students recognize state-of-being verbs, and to help them distinguish the state-of-being verb from the action verb. The meanings of several state-of-being verbs other than *to be* are explained. Students also practice using the various forms of the verb *to be* correctly. In Chapter 12, students will study sentence patterns in which the state-of-being verb is used as a linking verb.

Chapter Goals
At the conclusion of Chapter 5, students are expected to:
- find state-of-being verbs in sentences;
- distinguish between action and state-of-being verbs in sentences;
- select the correct form of the verb *to be*.

Vocabulary
active (6)	radish (6)
distinguish (6)	subject (5)
pudding (5)	tense (6)

Teaching Suggestions
1. Discuss the meaning, pronunciation, and spelling of each vocabulary word. Remind students that the subject of a sentence is the person or thing that is being talked about.
2. Discuss the introductory information and examples. Have students complete the Warm-Up exercises.

Lesson 1. What Is a State-of-Being Verb?
Overview
The activities in Lesson 1 develop the concept of state-of-being. Students learn to recognize state-of-being verbs and to identify the tense of the verbs used in sentences.

Lesson Goals
At the conclusion of this lesson, students are expected to:
- find verbs and verb phrases in sentences;
- differentiate action and state-of-being verbs.

Vocabulary
absent (5)	passive (10)
conditional (8)	phrase (6)
exist (6)	progressive (7)
infinitive	snack (6)

Teaching Suggestions
1. Discuss the lesson objectives with the students.
2. Be sure that students know the meaning of the vocabulary words. The word *exist* is especially important to the state-of-being concept.
3. Discuss the introductory information and examples.
4. Have students complete the lesson activities.
5. Discuss the information at the bottom of page 111. Students should understand that *to be* can be a helping verb, and it can also be used as a main verb.

Follow-Up Activity
Find a short passage in a literature book, magazine, or newspaper. Have students locate the verb or verb phrase in each sentence. Each time that the verb *to be* is used, have students decide whether it is a helping verb or a main verb.

Lesson 2. Action or State-of-Being?
Overview
In Lesson 2, several state-of-being verbs are defined and distinguished from their meanings when used as action verbs.

Lesson Goals
At the conclusion of Lesson 2, students are expected to:
- locate the verb or verb phrase in sentences;
- determine whether the verb expresses action or state-of-being.

Vocabulary
cranberry (5)	odor (6)
cultivate (6)	physical (7)
exist (6)	substitute (6)
existence (6)	visible (5)
mental (5)	

Teaching Suggestions

1. Discuss the information on page 115-116 with the class.
2. Discuss the meanings of the verbs presented; then, do the exercises as a group.
3. Most of the new vocabulary appear in the definitions of the verbs. Be sure students understand the meaning of the vocabulary words as well as the definitions of the verbs in the lesson.
4. Tell students that in most cases we can determine if a verb expresses a state-of-being by substituting a form of the verb to be for the verb in question.

Follow-Up Activity

Divide the class into pairs or groups of three. Assign each pair/group one of the eight verbs presented in Activity B. Have them make up several sentences using the verb as an action verb and a state-of-being verb. Use the sentences to conduct additional drills. Students can read the sentences; others can try to identify the verb as either action or state-of-being.

Lesson 3. Using State-of-Being Verbs
Overview

In Lesson 3, students review the subject-verb agreement rule. The various forms of the verb to be are presented and some common usage mistakes are explained. Students practice using the correct forms of the verb in sentences.

Lesson Goal

At the conclusion of the lesson, students are expected to select correct forms of the verb to be.

Vocabulary

conditional (8)	neuter (11)
extremely (7)	participle
feminine (7)	plural (6)
infinitive	progressive (7)
irregular (7)	singular (8)
masculine (7)	

Teaching Suggestions

1. Only one of the vocabulary words above is introduced for the first time — extremely.

Review all of the terms and point them out in the text as the lesson is presented.
2. Review the masculine (he), feminine (she), and neuter (it) forms of the third person singular pronoun.
3. Remind students that the past participle form of the verb is used to form the perfect tenses and always includes a form of the verb to have in the verb phrase.
4. Remind students that the present participle always ends in -ing. With a form of the verb to be, it is used to express the progressive verb form.
5. Discuss the information and examples on pages 120-122. Have students complete the exercises.
6. Discuss the common mistakes on page 123 and have students complete Activity D.

Follow-Up Activities

1. Have students develop a chart from memory using the verb to be in all three persons, singular and plural, and in all six tenses.
2. Divide the class into small groups and have each group write ten sentences using the verb to be correctly. Tell them that be can be a helping verb or a main verb.

Chapter Review

Prior to assigning the Chapter Review on page 125, conduct the review activity below. Follow-Up activities can be used now or repeated as necessary.

Review Activity

Have students write several sentences about a person they know or a public person. Tell them to use only state-of-being verbs. The sentences will tell something about the person, rather than anything about what the person is doing or has done. Students should underline each verb/verb phrase and share their sentences with the class.

Answer Key for Chapter 5
Warm-Up A

1. is	4. is
2. is looking	5. has been keeping
3. has felt	

Warm-Up B
1. appeared - action
2. appears - being
3. felt - action
4. felt - being
5. looked - action
6. seemed - being
7. grew - being
8. grow - action

Lesson 1, pages 111-114
Activity A
Sentences will vary.

Activity B
1. was feeling - helping
2. is - main
3. is going - helping
4. will be - main
5. will be - main
6. was given - helping (passive)

Activity C
1. is - present
2. will be - future
3. has been - present perfect
4. was - past
5. had been - past perfect
6. will have been - future perfect

Activity D
Sentences will vary.

Lesson Review
1. were
2. would taste
3. smelled
4. looked
5. Is
6. was
7. have been
8. was
9. is

Lesson 2, pages 115-119
Activity A
1. action
2. being
3. being
4. action
5. action
6. being
7. being
8. action
9. being
10. action

Activity B
Answers will vary.

Activity C
1. state-of-being
2. action
3. state-of-being
4. state-of-being
5. state-of-being
6. action
7. action
8. state-of-being
9. action
10. state-of-being

Activity D
1. was served - action (passive)
2. looked - being
3. is looking - being
4. want - action
5. tasted - being
6. will have - action
7. looked - being
8. am getting - being (*get* means *become* in this sentence)
9. will be - being
10. was - being

Lesson Review
1. was looking - action
2. keeps - action
3. gets - being
4. appeared - action
5. was - being
6. appeared - being
7. looked - being
8. got - action
9. grew - being
10. relaxed - action
11. was damaged - action (passive)
12. remained - action
13. got - action

Lesson 3, pages 120-124
Activity A
1. am
2. were
3. was
4. were
5. was
6. was
7. were
8. is
9. is
10. are

Activity B
1. is
2. was
3. were
4. been
5. is
6. being
7. are
8. been

Activity C
Be should be used in all of the sentences.

Activity D
1. Where *is* Roberto?
2. He *is* at football practice.
3. They *are* practicing late.
4. We *are* going to the drugstore after school.
5. He *will* be here soon.

Lesson Review

1.	be	9.	was
2.	is	10.	be
3.	be	11.	was (is)*
4.	is (was)*	12.	be
5.	are (were)*	13.	was (is)*
6.	were	14.	were (are)*
7.	was	15.	was (is)*
8.	been	16.	was (is)*

*Answers may vary depending on how the students interpret the time frame of the story.

Chapter Review
Part A

1.	grew	6.	was
2.	felt	7.	was

3.	were growing	8.	would come
4.	became	9.	was feeling
5.	smelled	10.	was

Part B
1. stayed - being
2. got - action
3. gets - being (complained - action)
4. looked - being
5. can smell - action (said - action)
6. feels - being (said - action)
7. felt - action (said - action)
8. looked - action

Part C
1. is
2. am
3. are
4. was
5. were
6. been
7. be
8. be

Chapter 6
The Adverb

Overview

Chapter 6 presents the adverb as a part of speech that modifies, or answers questions about the verb, adjectives, and other adverbs in a sentence. Comparisons are explained in one lesson; other usage problems are addressed in the final lesson.

Chapter Goal

At the conclusion of the chapter, students are expected to identify all types of adverbs in sentences.

Vocabulary

comparison (6)   negation
contraction (9)   negative (8)
extremely (6)   versatile (11)
irregular (7)

Teaching Suggestions

1. Discuss the vocabulary words before beginning the Warm-Up exercises.
2. Discuss the introductory information. Have students find the verbs in the example sentences. Stress that the adverb answers a question about the verb.
3. Discuss the adverbs of degree. Stress that these adverbs also answer questions.
4. Use the Warm-Up exercises either as a pretest or an introductory oral exercise.
5. If necessary, review the information about comparative forms of adjectives. Tell students that the same rules generally apply to adverbs.

Lesson 1. Adverbs That Modify Verbs
Overview

Lesson 1 presents adverbs that modify verbs. Adverbs of manner, which answer the question, *how?*, adverbs of time, which answer the question, *when?*, and adverbs of place, which answer the question, *where?*, are all introduced.

Lesson Goal

At the conclusion of the lesson, students are expected to be able to identify adverbs in sentences.

Vocabulary

advance (5)   graceful (6)
assignment (6)   hem (6)
ballerina   occasionally (6)
constant (6)   relative (5)

Teaching Suggestions

1. Be sure students can spell and pronounce the vocabulary words. Have students divide the words into syllables.
2. Discuss the introductory information and examples.
3. Have students complete activities independently. Discuss the answers and identify the verbs in each sentence.

Follow-Up Activities

1. Use the sentences that the students develop for Activity C on page 131 for additional oral drills.
2. Have students find pictures in magazines that illustrate the following adverbs: gracefully, smoothly, slowly, happily, loudly, fast, cautiously.

Lesson 2. Adverbs of Degree
Overview

In Lesson 2, students develop the concept of degree and practice finding and using adverbs of degree in sentences.

Lesson Goals

At the conclusion of the lesson, students are expected to:
• identify adverbs of degree in sentences;
• add appropriate adverbs of degree to sentences containing either an adverb or an adjective.

Vocabulary

tennis (5)

Teaching Suggestions

1. Discuss the introductory information. Stress that the adverb of degree usually comes before the adjective or adverb that it modifies.

There are certain expressions in which the adverb of degree follows the adjective, such as, that house is *big enough for us*. *Enough* modifies *big*.

2. Students should complete the activities independently. Then, discuss the correct answers with the class.

Follow-Up Activity

Have students develop additional sentences using adverbs of degree.

Lesson 3. Recognizing Adverbs
Overview

Lesson 3 provides additional practice recognizing adverbs. Student distinguish adverbs from adjectives and learn how adverbs are formed from adjectives and nouns by adding *-ly*.

Lesson Goal

At the end of Lesson 3, students are expected to distinguish between adverbs and adjectives in sentences.

Vocabulary

alphabetical (6)	definition (6)
costly (6)	strychnine

Teaching Suggestions

1. Discuss the vocabulary words, emphasizing pronunciation.
2. Discuss the introductory information and conduct Activity A orally. Read the remaining information with the group and have students do the activities independently.

Follow-Up Activity

Have students use the words listed below in sentences. Be sure they can identify the part of speech correctly. Do this either as a written or oral activity.

Adjectives	Adverbs
accidental	accidentally
accurate	accurately
active	actively
beautiful	beautifully
brave	bravely
cautious	cautiously

confident	confidently
dreadful	dreadfully
exact	exactly
guilt	guiltily
heavy	heavily
kind	kindly
meek	meekly
prompt	promptly
regular	regularly
selfish	selfishly
sharp	sharply
tender	tenderly
warm	warmly

Lesson 4. Comparing Adverbs
Overview

Students practice writing the positive, comparative, and superlative forms of the adverb. Usage rules are also discussed.

Lesson Goals

At the conclusion of Lesson 4, students are expected to:
• locate adverbs in sentences;
• identify the degree of comparison.

Vocabulary

choir (5)	comparison (6)
chorus (5)	positive (6)
comparative	superlative (10)

Teaching Suggestions

1. Provide students with a list of adverbs divided into syllables. Be sure to include several one-syllable words. All of these adverbs should be in the positive form.
2. Discuss the information on page 141. Remind students of the rules for comparing with adjectives (Chapter 3, Lesson 6), and tell them the adverb is compared in the same manner.
3. Point out that we often use *the* with superlative forms:
    He writes *best* about football.
    He writes *the best* about football.
    Ordinarily, a word following the article is a noun; however, *best* is an adverb.
4. Point out that most two-syllable adverbs form their comparative and superlative forms by

using the words *more* and *most* or *less* and *least*. However, there are exceptions, such as *early, earlier, earliest*.

5. Explain that not all adverbs are used to make comparative statements. For example: *More completely* and *most completely* are illogical. *More today* and *most today* are illogical. Adverbs of degree do not have comparative and superlative forms.

6. After the activities in the lesson are completed, have students identify the degree of comparison in each sentence.

Follow-Up Activity

Divide the class into pairs or small groups and have each group develop a list of adverbs. Tell them to write the positive, comparative, and superlative forms. Provide each group with a dictionary to assist them in the activity.

Lesson 5. Using Adverbs Correctly
Overview

In Lesson 5, students practice using adverbs correctly. They are instructed to make the adverb of time and the verb tense agree. The difference between *good* and *well* is explained.

Lesson Goal

At the conclusion of the lesson, students are expected to identify usage errors in sentences and to correct them.

Teaching Suggestions

1. Discuss the introductory information. Stress that the tense of the verb and the adverb of time must agree.

2. Activities A and B may be done orally to ensure that students have an understanding.

Follow-Up Activity

Have students write sentences using *good* and *well* to ensure that students have an understanding.

Chapter Review

Do any follow-up activities that were omitted earlier; then, use the review activities below. Students should not identify adjectives as adverbs when they complete the Chapter Review. No more than five errors are permitted to demonstrate mastery of the chapter objective.

Review Activities

1. Have students develop sentences using adjectives and adverbs. Use the sentences as a drill. Each student should read a sentence and specify a word. The class should identify the word as either an adverb or an adjective. For example:
    Student: We arrived early. What part of speech is *early*?
    Response: *Early* is an adverb.

2. Select a short paragraph from a literature book, newspaper, or magazine. Have students read each sentence aloud and identify the adverbs and the adjectives.

3. Have each student write several sentences about a recent event, using as many adverbs as possible. Then, have the students exchange papers and locate the adverbs.

Answer Key for Chapter 6
Warm-Up A

1.	carefully	4.	too
2.	everywhere	5.	almost
3.	very, yesterday	6.	away, today

Warm-Up B

1.	not	4.	never
2.	n't	5.	never
3.	not		

Warm-Up C

1.	fastest	3.	better
2.	more slowly	4.	less quickly

Lesson 1, pages 130-133
Activity A

Answers will vary.
Suggested answers are:

1. quickly, hungrily
2. carefully, fast, slowly
3. well, nicely
4. carefully, slowly
5. sweetly, loudly
6. thoroughly, fast, well

Activity B
1. gracefully
2. carefully
3. gladly
4. Slowly
5. hard
6. well
7. quickly
8. fast
9. happily
10. straight

Activity C
Answers will vary.

Activity D
1. immediately
2. first
3. instantly
4. ago
5. before
6. lately
7. Sometimes
8. Occasionally
9. daily
10. yearly

Activity E
1. forward
2. away
3. right
4. here
5. upstairs
6. above
7. near

Lesson Review
1. Yesterday, carelessly
2. loudly
3. always, angrily
4. never, again
5. up, down, constantly
6. not
7. Finally
8. quickly
9. away, happily
10. now

Lesson 2, pages 134-136
Activity A
1. very
2. too
3. so
4. unusually

Activity B
1. almost
2. rather
3. too
4. quite
5. completely
6. extremely

Activity C
1. very
2. too
3. unusually
4. sometime
5. far
6. much
7. somewhat

Activity D
Answers may vary.
Suggested answers are:
1. extremely (strong)
2. almost (ready)
3. very (pretty)
4. unusually (well)
5. quite (often)
6. too (quickly)

Activity E
Answers will vary.

Lesson Review
Part A
1. very
2. completely
3. extremely
4. unusually
5. very
6. quite

Part B
Answers will vary. The adverb or adjective is:
1. cold
2. warmly
3. bare
4. cloudy
5. Soon
6. ready, tomorrow

Lesson 3, pages 137-140
Activity A
1. adjective
2. adverb
3. adjective
4. adverb
5. adjective
6. adverb
7. adverb
8. adverb
9. adverb
10. adverb
11. adverb
12. adjective
13. adjective
14. adjective
15. adverb
16. adverb
17. adjective
18. adverb
19. adjective
20. adverb

Activity B

1. adjective
2. adverb
3. adjective
4. adverb
5. adverb
6. adjective
7. adjective
8. adverb

Activity C

1. noun
2. adverb
3. noun
4. adverb
5. noun
6. adverb

Activity D

1. adjective
2. adjective
3. adjective
4. adverb
5. adjective

Lesson Review

1. adjective
2. adjective
3. adverb
4. adverb
5. adverb
6. adverb
7. adverb
8. adjective
9. adjective
10. adjective

Lesson 4, pages 141-143
Activity A

1. comfortably
2. more comfortably
3. most comfortably
4. calmly
5. more calmly
6. most calmly
7. well
8. better
9. best

Activity B

1. more loudly, most loudly
2. more brightly, most brightly
3. faster, fastest
4. harder, hardest
5. more gladly, most gladly
6. more clearly, most clearly
7. more softly, most softly
8. more angrily, most angrily

Activity C

1. brightly
2. better
3. harder*
4. most quickly
5. more loudly

*The implication is that Dan works is two situations - when he is interested and when he isn't.

Lesson Review

1. faster - comparative
2. hard - positive
3. best - superlative
4. less quickly - comparative
5. more loudly - comparative
6. least happily - superlative
7. better - comparative
8. most loudly - superlative
9. more quietly - comparative
10. well - positive

Lesson 5, pages 144-145
Activity A

1. went (ago is past)
2. were (yesterday is past)
3. will arrive (soon implies future)
4. had painted (before suggested the action was completed in the past);
   have painted or painted are acceptable alternative answers.
5. is eating (now implies the action is going on in the present.)

Activity B

1. gracefully
2. happily
3. loudly
4. quickly
5. quietly

Activity C

1. good
2. well
3. good
4. well
5. well is preferred; good is also acceptable

Lesson Review

1. were
2. quickly
3. well
4. better
5. is speaking
6. softly

Chapter Review

1. early (When?)
2. very*
3. somewhat*
   patiently (How?)
4. early (When?)

5. not (Negation)
   so*
6. anyway (How?)
7. extremely*
8. never (Negation)
9. probably (How?)
   very*
10. unusually*
11. more*
    slowly (or more slowly) (How?)
12. Finally (When?)

13. carefully (How?)
14. almost*
15. excitedly (How?)
16. quickly (How?)
17. Soon (When?)
18. still (When?)
19. already (When?)
    outside (Where?)
20. here (Where?)
*Adverbs of degree

Chapter 7
The Preposition

Overview

The purpose of Chapter 7 is to help students recognize and use prepositional phrases. Lesson 1 introduces the preposition, while Lessons 2 and 3 deal with prepositional phrases used as adjectives and adverbs. The final lesson explains rules regarding the object of the preposition.

Chapter Goals

At the conclusion of the chapter, students are expected to:
- identify prepositional phrases as either adjective or adverb phrases;
- locate prepositional phrases in sentences;
- add prepositional phrases to sentences;
- distinguish the prepositional phrase from the infinitive.

Vocabulary

adverb	phrase (6)
adjective	preposition
bored (5)	prepositional phrase
concert (5)	relationship (6)

Teaching Suggestions

1. Discuss all vocabulary words, emphasizing the definitions of adjectives and adverbs.
2. Discuss the introductory information on pages 147-149. Then, conduct the chapter Warm-Up exercises.

Follow-Up Activities

1. Review the meaning of the term *phrase* — a group of words (two or more) acting together. Tell the students to make a list of phrases, and then to write several short sentences. Using the students' work, select either a phrase or a sentence at random. Students should identify the selection as either a phrase or a sentence.
2. Conduct any of the Follow-Up activities suggested for Chapters 3 and 6 to refresh the students knowledge of adjectives and adverbs. These should be done before beginning the lessons in this chapter.

Lesson 1. Understanding Prepositions
Overview

Lesson 1 is designed to develop the concept of a preposition as a part of speech that expresses a relationship between a word (the object of the preposition) and another part of the sentence. Emphasize that a preposition always has an object, which is part of the prepositional phrase.

Lesson Goal

At the conclusion of Lesson 1, students are expected to locate prepositions and prepositional phrases in sentences.

Vocabulary

phrase (6)	relationship (6)
preposition	underneath (5)
prepositional	vote (5)

Teaching Suggestions

1. Review the meanings of the terms *phrase*, *preposition*, and *prepositional phrase*. Be sure students know the meanings of the other vocabulary words used in the lesson.
2. Discuss the information of page 135 and conduct Activity A orally.
3. Conduct as many of the activities orally as is practical, pointing out the cadence of the prepositional phrase. (The preposition is usually lightly stressed. The object receives a heavier stress.)
4. In each activity, indicate the word in the sentence the prepositional phrase is modifying.

Follow-Up Activity

Conduct a pantomime to demonstrate how prepositions change the meaning of a sentence. One student will pantomime and the others will try to guess the preposition used in the sentence. For example: John (the person doing the pantomime) is walking *into* the room, *across* the room, *out* of the room, etc.

Each student may write five prepositions to use during his or her pantomime. The teacher should demonstrate the activity before the students take a turn. Be sure all of the guesses are expressed in prepositional phrases. To get full benefit from the activity, the students should hear the phrases spoken. For example:

Teacher: I am putting this book ...
Students: ...*on* your desk, *in* your desk, etc.

Lesson 2. The Prepositional Phrase Used as an Adjective
Overview
This lesson will help students recognize prepositional phrases that are used as adjectives in sentences.

Lesson Goals
At the conclusion of Lesson 2, students are expected to:
• identify prepositional phrases in sentences;
• identify the noun or pronoun that the phrase describes.

Vocabulary

applauded (6)	mail
auditorium (5)	poem (5)
establish (5)	population (5)
headquarters (6)	spruce (6)

Teaching Suggestions
1. Present and discuss the vocabulary words, all of which are used in the activities. Students should know the meanings, spellings, and pronunciations of these words.
2. Review the meaning of the word adjective before discussing the information and examples.
3. If at all possible, conduct the activities as oral exercises. Stress the cadence of the prepositional phrase as a means of identification.

Follow-Up Activities
1. Tell the students to write a list of nouns or pronouns. Then, have them write a prepositional phrase that describes each word on their lists.
2. Have the students select one noun and one pronoun from their lists. Tell them to write five prepositional phrases about each of the words. Be sure the noun they select is not the name of a person.

Lesson 3. The Prepositional Phrase Used as an Adverb
Overview
This lesson will help students recognize prepositional phrase used as adverbs in sentences.

Lesson Goal
At the end of Lesson 3, students are expected to identify prepositional phrases used as adverbs in sentences.

Vocabulary

accounting (5)	program (4)
computer (8)	programmer
industry (6)	pudding (5)
install (6)	technology

Teaching Suggestions
1. Review the meaning of the word adverb reminding students that adverbs usually answer the questions *where?*, *when?*, *why?*, and *how?* When the prepositional phrase is used as an adverb, it answers the same questions as an adverb about a verb in a sentence.
2. Go over the information and examples on pages 158-159.
3. Assign the activities and discuss the correct answers.

Follow-Up Activities
1. Tell students to write five verbs, and then supply a prepositional phrase after each. For example:
     travel - to the beach
     jump-   over the fence
2. Have the students select one verb and write several prepositional phrases for that verb. For example:
     travel - through the woods
               to Florida
               on an airplane
               for several weeks
               because of my job

Lesson 4. The Object of the Preposition
Overview
This lesson will help students distinguish infinitives from prepositional phrases and from verb

forms using *to*. In addition it will help them recognize objects of the preposition that are verbals. The object of the preposition as a pronoun is also discussed.

Lesson Goals
At the conclusion of this lesson, students are expected to:
- recognize prepositional phrases in sentences;
- distinguish an infinitive from a prepositional phrase.

Vocabulary
computer (6)	gerund
concentrate (5)	infinitive
confidence (5)	mathematics (6)
education (5)	

Teaching Suggestions
1. Discuss the vocabulary words. Review the meanings of the words *infinitive* and *gerund*. Remind students that these words are *verbals* —verb forms used as other parts of speech.
2. Review the list of helping verbs used with conditional forms on page 102.
3. Review the objective and nominative forms of the personal pronouns in Chapter 2. Explain that the object of the preposition must be in the objective case of the pronoun.
4. The most common position for the preposition is before its object. In actual speech, however, the prepositional phrase does not always follow the word it modifies, nor does the preposition always precede the word it governs.

Follow-Up Activity
Select a passage from a literature book, newspaper, or magazine. Students should read each sentence aloud, identify the prepositional phrases, and decide whether each phrase is used as an adjective or an adverb.

Chapter Review
Prior to assigning the Chapter Review on page 166, conduct any follow-up activities that were omitted earlier. To have mastered this topic, students should make no more than one error in each part. Use the activities below as desired.

Review Activities
1. Have students list at least 25 prepositions and develop a word search puzzle. Then, tell them to make a second copy and circle all of the words that they included in their puzzle. Students may exchange the puzzles and locate the prepositions.
2. Make a list of prepositions and divide the list among groups of students. Each group should look up each word on the list in a dictionary and develop an entry in their own words. Tell students to include a sentence using each preposition. Prepare a class dictionary of definitions.
3. Assign a topic to the class or allow students to choose their own. Tell students to list several sentences about the topic, underlining all of the prepositional phrases.

Answer Key for Chapter 7
Warm-Up A
1. across the street
2. under a tree
3. at the dog
4. down the sidewalk
5. with the other dog

Warm-Up B
1.	adjective	6.	adverb
2.	adjective, adverb	7.	adverb
3.	adverb	8.	adjective
4.	adverb	9.	adverb
5.	adjective, adverb	10.	adjective

Warm-Up C
1.	adverb	5.	adverb
2.	preposition	6.	preposition
3.	adverb	7.	adverb
4.	preposition	8.	preposition

Lesson 1, pages 150-154
Activity A
Answers will vary.
Possible answers are:
1. on, under
2. on, next to
3. by
4. in

5. on, in, under
6. of, in
7. with, of
8. with
9. beside, across from, next to, with
10. on

Activity B
Answers will vary.

Activity C
1. at the store
2. of sentences
3. across the clear blue lake
4. near a very busy highway
5. with me
6. in the left-hand corner
7. to him
8. Around the corner
9. with ice cream
10. of the city
11. for him
12. in North Carolina
13. to Tennessee
14. during a heavy storm
15. to me

Activity D
1.	adverb	5.	adverb
2.	preposition	6.	preposition
3.	adverb	7.	adverb
4.	adverb	8.	preposition

Activity E
Answers will vary.

Activity F
1.	According to Joe	4.	out of the house
2.	instead of Tim	5.	along with us
3.	in place of Judy	6.	in front of Karl

Lesson Review
1.	for his final exams	5.	around the corner
2.	in his room	6.	in ten minutes
3.	on the telephone	7.	for me
4.	from you	8.	In spite of his trouble

Lesson 2, pages 155-157
Activity A
1. homework
2. boy
3. flowers
4. house
5. None
6. All
7. poem

Activity B
1. The story by John Steinbeck
2. the tickets for football
3. day in spring
4. ring with diamonds
5. map of the city
6. light on the porch
7. boots for skiing
8. table in the kitchen
9. homework in (for) English
10. house of brick

Activity C
1. in the woods, beside the lake
2. in a store, in Marshall Mall
3. to Yellowstone Park, in Wyoming
4. on the table, in your room
5. of the people, in the auditorium

Activity D
Answers will vary.
A sample response for item #1 is:
Everyone at Wilson High likes the football games on Saturdays.

Lesson Review
1. in January - Alaska
2. throughout the state - spruces
3. of Alaska - history
4. of Alaska - explorer
5. from Russia - People
6. in Sitka - headquarters
7. in the United States - state
8. of our last frontiers - one
9. of Alaska - population
10. of Alaska - study

Lesson 3, pages 158-161
Activity A
1. When?	9. Where?
2. Where?	10. How?
3. Where?	11. Where?
4. When?	12. Where?
5. When?	13. Where?
6. Where?	14. How?
7. How?	15. Where?
8. How?	

Activity B
1. because of the rain
2. for English class
3. for her family
4. for the salad
5. for himself
6. for me
7. because of his fever

Activity C
1. in the trash can
2. on the first floor, in the building
3. with her mother, at the store
4. for the family's groceries
5. from the fire

Activity D
Answers will vary.

Lesson Review
1. at Hanover Community College
2. for two years
3. in accounting
4. in a bank
5. in almost every industry
6. in business firms, in 1951
7. for recordkeeping
8. At school, with diskettes or tapes
9. for information
10. about computer languages
11. with computer languages
12. for the computer
13. with computers
14. in the field

Lesson 4, pages 162-165
Activity A
1. prepositional phrase
2. infinitive
3. prepositional phrase
4. infinitive
5. infinitive
6. prepositional phrase, infinitive
7. prepositional phrase
8. infinitive
9. prepositional phrase
10. prepositional phrase

Activity B
Answers will vary.

Activity C
1. with her friend	4. for everyone
2. on it	5. between them
3. by himself	6. with this

Activity D
1. for Jack and me
2. for himself
3. to everyone
4. Between the two of them

Activity E
1. about whom
2. with whom
3. with which
4. for which
5. for what

Activity F
1. of Mary Lyon
2. in the education
3. of women
4. in 1797
5. in 1849
6. in schools
7. in New Hampshire
8. in Massachusetts
9. In those days
10. for middle-class women

11. in 1837
12. in Massachusetts
13. of the school
14. about mathematics, science, and Latin
15. except to teach
16. of everyone
17. through her work
18. in themselves

Lesson Review
1. in a bank
2. with computers
3. for a test
4. with Patrick and Mike
5. to everyone
6. except to concentrate
7. for the test, by studying
8. on his paper
9. What - for
10. with the test
11. to the teacher, of relief

Chapter Review
Part A
1. adjective (Which one?)
2. adjective (Which one?)
3. adverb (Why?)
4. adverb (When?)
5. adverb (Why?)

Part B
1. for a minute
2. in a yellow sports car
3. for dinner
4. for everyone
5. with clean-up

Part C
Answers will vary.

Chapter 8
The Conjunction

Overview
Chapter 8 presents conjunctions as words that connect ideas in sentences. Students learn the three types of conjunctions: *coordinating, subordinating,* and *correlative.*

Chapter Goals
At the conclusion of Chapter 8, students are expected to:
* identify conjunctions in sentences;
* punctuate sentences with conjunctions;
* add appropriate conjunctions to sentences.

Vocabulary
absent (5)	spaghetti (5)
conjunction	spices (5)
connect (5)	subordinate (9)
hockey (5)	tennis (5)
mileage (7)	vanilla (6)
phrase (6)	

Teaching Suggestions
1. Explain that conjunctions connect parts of sentences. Sometimes the parts are equal, or independent, such as two subjects, two verbs, or two complete sentences. Other times a conjunction connects a subordinate clause with an independent clause (sentence). A subordinate is something that is placed below something else in rank or importance. In grammar, it is a clause that is dependent on another clause to make sense.
2. Point out the vocabulary words as they are encountered in the Warm-Up activities. Have students learn all the words.
3. Use the Warm-Up activities as a pretest if desired.

Lesson 1. Coordinating Conjunctions
Overview
Lesson 1 presents the coordinating conjunction, the rules for punctuating words or phrases in a series, as well as compound sentences. Prepositions and conjunctions are compared.

Lesson Goals
At the conclusion of Lesson 1, students are expected to:
* identify coordinating conjunctions in sentences;
* punctuate sentences with conjunctions.

Vocabulary
communicate (5)	petunia
consequently (8)	poetry (6)
coordinating (9)	preposition
daffodil	pudding
equipment (5)	punctuate (7)
furthermore (6)	referee (6)
hamburger (5)	relax (5)
hockey (5)	restaurant (5)
manager (6)	series (5)
moreover	spinach
nevertheless	steak (5)
otherwise (5)	strawberry (6)
tulip (5)	

Teaching Suggestions
1. Review all words in the vocabulary list.
2. The term *coordinate* means to arrange so that the items are equal in rank. In grammar, a coordinating conjunction joins equal elements to produce a compound element.
3. Discuss the meanings of conjunctions as they appear throughout the lesson.

Follow-Up Activities
1. Have the students use the conjunctions listed on page 173 in original sentences.
2. Locate a brief selection in a literature book, magazine, or newspaper. Have the students read each sentence aloud and identify the conjunctions.
3. Tell the students to make lists of the following items: two or more nouns, two or more verbs, two or more adjectives, two or more adverbs, two or more prepositional phrases, and two or more pronouns. Then, have them write a sentence, using a conjunction to join each of these pairs of series of words.

Lesson 2. Subordinating Conjunctions
Overview
Lesson 2 introduces the subordinating conjunctions, the subordinate or dependent clause, and the rules for punctuation with these elements. Prepositions and conjunctions are also compared.

Lesson Goals
At the conclusion of Lesson 2, students are expected to:
• connect pairs of sentences using subordinating conjunctions;
• punctuate sentences with subordinating conjunctions.

Vocabulary
clause (7)	election (5)
college (5)	gain (5)
computer (8)	independent (6)
dependent (7)	subordinating (9)
wrestling (5)	vote (5)

Teaching Suggestions
1. Explain that the subordinating conjunction introduces a clause that is not a complete idea; it must accompany an independent clause to make sense. For example:
I am late is a complete sentence. If we place a subordinating conjunction before that sentence, we create a dependent clause. *Because I am late* is not a complete idea.
2. Present the words *dependent* and *independent* to the class and explain their opposite meanings.
3. Discuss the meanings of all of the subordinating conjunctions used in this lesson.

Follow-Up Activities
1. Tell the students to look up these words in a dictionary, find their meaning as conjunctions, then, use each in a sentence: after, although, as, because, if, since, so, unless, where, while.
2. Divide the class into groups. Each group should write several pairs of sentences and then connect the pairs using a subordinating conjunction. Next, have the student write sentences on the chalkboard. Other students should identify the dependent clauses.

Lesson 3. Correlative Conjunctions
Overview
Lesson 3 presents the conjunctions that are used in pairs. Subject-verb agreement is also explained.

Lesson Goals
At the conclusion of this lesson, students are expected to:
• identify correlative conjunctions in sentences;
• select the correct verb form in sentences with correlative conjunctions.

Vocabulary
correlate (2)	re-run
correlative	satisfactory (6)
due (5)	subject (5)
perfume (5)	

Teaching Suggestions
1. Explain that correlative conjunctions express a shared relationship and are always used in pairs to join equal parts in a sentence. For example:
"Neither Ted nor Andy enjoyed that movie," means that Ted didn't enjoy the movie, and Andy didn't enjoy the movie.
2. When the correlative conjunction joins a pair of subjects, there may be a problem with subject-verb agreement. Point out that in some cases a correct sentence may sound awkward. For example:
Correct — Not only the house, but also the garage needs painting.
Better — The house as well as the garage needs painting.
Sometimes a correct sentence is awkward and should be revised.

Follow-Up Activity
Students should now be able to recognize all kinds of conjunctions in sentences. Assign a topic so that students can write a short paragraph. Tell them to use conjunctions and underline them. Some suggested topics are:
1. A Not-So Famous Person
2. The Craziest Animal I Ever Knew
3. A Skill I Wish I Had and Why

Chapter Review

Before beginning the Chapter Review, discuss the three types of conjunctions. Use any follow-up activities previously omitted, or repeat those that would be useful at this point.

Vocabulary

approve (5)
disc jockey
slacks (6)

Review Activities

1. Locate a selection in a literature book, magazine, or newspaper. Read each sentence aloud with the group. Students should identify all conjunctions.
2. Write different conjunctions or pairs of conjunctions on slips of paper. Have each student draw a word (or phrase) and use it in a sentence as a conjunction. The class should judge whether the word has been used correctly. Tell students to note sentences in which the conjunction is used as a preposition instead of a conjunction.

Answer Key for Chapter 8
Warm-Up A

1. and
2. or
3. if
4. but
5. because
6. however
7. Either ... or
8. not only ... but also
9. whether ... or
10. and
11. but
12. and
13. After
14. Unless

Warm-Up B

Answers will vary.

Lesson 1, pages 170-175
Activity A

1. and
2. and
3. and
4. but
5. or
6. for

Activity B

Sample Answers:
1. Carol and Lance like ice cream.
2. Todd plays football and baseball.
3. Edgar Allen Poe wrote short stories and poetry.
4. I grew tomatoes and green beans in my garden.
5. Laura likes basketball and hockey.

Activity C

Answers will vary.

Activity D

1. bushes, trees, and
2. tulips, daffodils, and
3. washed up, changed our clothes, and
4. hamburger, french fries, and
5. ice cream, pie, cake, or
6. but
7. apple, cherry, and

Activity E

Answers will vary.

Activity F

1. hurry; otherwise,
2. shopping; instead,
3. book, ... homework, ... TV, and ... relaxed.
4. school, but
5. steak, but
6. trees; furthermore,
7. stories; also,
8. ice cream, but

Activity G

1. conjunction
2. conjunction
3. preposition
4. preposition

Lesson Review

1. where (no punctuation)
2. Antoinette, but
3. first, for
4. better; therefore,
5. or (no punctuation)
6. Toni; furthermore,

Lesson 2, pages 176-179
Activity A
1. If you are gaining weight
2. until I finish
3. in order that he could go to college
4. When Lisa gets here
5. while they watched the movie
6. as the crow flies

Activity B
Answers will vary.

Activity C
Answers will vary.

Activity D
1. Zack is lifting weights because he wants to be on the wrestling team.
2. Pete went to the library because he needed a book.
3. Sue is in Becky's English class since she moved to town in March.
4. While I was asleep, a storm blew down our tree.
5. Since you will drive today, I will drive tomorrow.

Activity E
1. preposition
2. conjunction
3. preposition
4. conjunction
5. preposition
6. conjunction
7. conjunction
8. preposition

Activity F
1. because
2. although
3. If
4. when
5. Where

Lesson Review
Part A , Sample Answers:
1. I made an A because I studied hard.
2. Since I will clean the house, you do the shopping.
3. When I get hungry about three o'clock, I eat an apple.
4. I can't go outside because the weather is too cold.
5. Since he didn't get enough votes, he lost the election.

Part B
1. *until* (no comma)
2. *If* you will help,
3. *When* warm weather arrives,
4. *Until* the team scored,
5. *as* (no comma)

Lesson 3, pages 180-182
Activity A
1. either . . . or
2. Both . . . and
3. Not only . . . but also
4. Neither . . . nor
5. whether . . . or
6. neither . . . nor

Activity B
1. is
2. are
3. is
4. is
5. makes

Lesson Review
1. Both . . . and
2. neither . . . nor
3. Not only . . . but also
4. either . . . or
5. whether . . . or

Chapter Review
Part A
1. and
2. whether . . . or
3. when
4. but , if
5. if
6. After
7. Either . . . or
8. but
9. neither . . . nor
10. If, and
11. If
12. because

Part B
1. Lisa, Anthony, Becky, and Todd
2. small, they
3. way, they
4. soon, we
5. band; however, they
6. arrived, they
7. dance, or
8. hungry, let's
9. good, and

Part C
Answers will vary. Suggested answers are:
1. After
2. but
3. Both . . . and
4. however
5. as well as
6. When
7. when
8. Not only . . . but

Chapter 9
The Interjection

Overview

Chapter 9 presents the final part of speech — the interjection. This chapter has only one lesson.

Chapter Goals

At the conclusion of Chapter 9, students are expected to:
- write sentences using an interjection in each;
- correctly punctuate sentences with interjections;
- capitalize the sentence after the interjection when necessary.

Vocabulary

bravo
capitalize (9)
emphasize (7)
exclamation (8)
interjection (11)
liver (6)

phrase (6)
punctuate (7)
punctuation (7)
related (6)
rip (5)

Teaching Suggestions

1. Present the vocabulary words that will be used in the chapter. Most interjections are not graded words. Although students should be familiar with words such as *hush, whew, ouch, yeah, ugh,* and so forth, they may have difficulty spelling and pronouncing them.
2. Discuss the information on page 185 and administer the Warm-Up activity on page 186. Much of the chapter material is suitable for oral discussion and responses. Students should share their lists of interjections.
3. Since all of the curse words are, of course, interjections, a discussion of socially acceptable and unacceptable language is appropriate for this lesson.

Follow-Up Activity

Students should recognize that interjections and exclamatory sentences are used sparingly in writing but more often in speech. Locate a dialogue in a literature book or magazine so that students can see examples of interjections in print. The comic strips are a good place to find examples of interjections in newspapers.

Answer Key for Chapter 9
Warm-Up

1. Wow! Isn't...
2. Ugh, we're...
3. Ouch! That...
4. Oh, no! I...
5. Whew! I...
6. Ugh, we're...

Lesson 1, pages 186-187
Activity A

Answers will vary.
Suggested answers are:

Oh, boy!
Aha!
Alas!
Hurray!
Whew!
Oh, my!
Ouch!
Stop!
Yeah!

Wow!
My goodness!
No way!
Ha!
Hey!
Aww!
Never!
Help!
Thanks!

Activity B

1. Quick! I need help fast!
2. Oh boy! What a great car!
3. Really? I didn't know that.
4. Well, you finally got here.
5. Oh no! You aren't giving me a shot.

Chapter Review

Answers will vary.

Part 2
Sentence Structure

Overview

Part 2 contains five chapters. Chapter 10 addresses the subject and the predicate in simple and compound sentences and explains the question and imperative sentence structures. Chapter 11 deals with basic sentence patterns and diagraming those patterns. Chapter 12 highlights sentence patterns with linking verbs. The complex sentence is introduced in Chapter 13. Students learn to identify adverb, noun, and adjective clauses. The appositive is also explained. The final chapter deals with the verbal and the verbal phrase. Infinitives, gerunds, and participles are discussed at length.

Part 2 Goals

At the conclusion of Part 2, students are expected to:
- identify the subject and the predicate in simple, compound, and complex sentences;
- distinguish between transitive and intransitive verbs;
- identify linking verbs and their complements;
- identify direct and indirect objects and objective complements;
- identify adverb, noun, and adjective clauses;
- identify infinitive, gerund, and participial phrases;
- evaluate sentences to determine whether they are correct or incorrect and then correct any errors;
- punctuate sentences correctly.

Teaching Suggestions

1. Skim through Part 2 with the class and discuss the overview and Part 2 goals above.
2. Begin each chapter by discussing explanations and examples.
3. Conduct all activities and discuss the answers with the class.
4. Use the words in the vocabulary as part of your instruction. Make sure that students can pronounce, spell, and define each word.

Introduction. What is a Sentence?
Overview

This introduction provides an overview to Part 2. Students are asked to demonstrate their knowledge of the sentence and its main parts. The major types of sentences (simple, compound, and complex) are explained and the purposes of sentences are discussed. Finally, the concept of sentence structure is introduced with an emphasis on transitive and intransitive verbs.

Introduction Goals

At the conclusion of the Introduction to Part 2, students are expected to:
- determine whether or not selected groups of words form sentences;
- identify the subject and the predicate parts of sentences;
- locate the simple and complete subjects and predicates in sentences;
- identify compound subjects and predicates in sentences;
- determine whether selected sentences are simple, compound, or complex;
- determine the purposes of selected sentences;
- determine whether verbs are transitive or intransitive.

Vocabulary

audience (5)	dependent (7)
auditorium (5)	hamburger (5)
barbecue (7)	include (5)
clause (7)	interrogative
communicate (6)	intransitive
complex (9)	predicate
complicated (7)	request (6)
compound (6)	subject (5)
concert (5)	transitive
conjunction	vibrations (6)

Teaching Suggestions

1. Discuss the overview and goals above.
2. Review the vocabulary words before beginning any activities. Most of the words will be familiar to the students; however, the words *predicate*, *transitive*, and *intransitive* should be introduced with emphasis.

3. Read the explanations and examples in the introduction and conduct each activity. Discuss all answers.

Follow-Up Activities
1. Use the activity sentences to review the eight parts of speech. Have students identify the parts of speech and provide a definition for each part.
2. Prepare about 50 index cards with one word on each card. Each of the eight parts of speech should be represented. Then, across the top of the chalkboard, write the names of the parts of speech. Now divide the class into two teams. One member of each team should draw a word from the stack, say the word aloud, and identify the part of speech. Finally, have the student use the word in a sentence as that part of speech. If the answer is correct, the team receives a point. If the answer is incorrect, a volunteer from the other team can attempt to identify and use the word. Continue until every member of the class has participated at least once.
   Example:
   Student (reading a card): But. This word is a preposition.
   Teacher: Use it in a sentence.
   Student: Everyone went but me.
   Teacher: Right. What other part of speech can this word be?
   Class: Conjunction.
3. Test the students' comprehension of sentence structure by writing a few simple sentences on the chalkboard. Include sentences with and without direct objects, with compound subjects and predicates, and with linking verbs and complements. Have students volunteer to write new sentences that follow the same pattern.

Answer Key for Introduction to Part 2
Pages 191-196
Activity A
1. Sentence
2. No
3. No
4. Sentence
5. Sentence
6. No
7. Sentence
8. Sentence

Activity B
1. Andy/ is looking at new cars.
2. Everyone at the party/ had a good time.
3. Brenda/ moved to town in March.
4. The whole family/planned a party for Mrs. Williams.
5. They all/ helped.

Activity C
1. Our (neighbor)
2. His whole (family)
3. The (color)
4. (They)
5. The (part) under the roof
6. The whole (job)

Activity D
1. was coming to town
2. bought two tickets
3. was on Saturday evening
4. decided to take Sue
5. enjoyed music very much
6. could feel the vibration of the band

Activity E
1. Compound predicate: went to the auditorium and got the tickets
2. Compound subject: Brenda and Bruce
3. Compound predicate: played their instruments and sang
4. Compound subject: Both the band and the audience

Activity F
1. simple
2. compound
3. complex
4. compound
5. complex

Activity G
1. question
2. statement
3. command
4. statement
5. question
6. statement
7. command
8. statement
9. question
10. command

Chapter 10
The Subject and the Predicate

Overview

Chapter 10 has three lessons that present the subject, the predicate, and the compound sentence. The major purpose is to develop the concept of the sentence as a group of words having two main parts that together express a complete thought.

Chapter Goals

At the conclusion of Chapter 10, students are expected to:
- identify the subject and the predicate parts of sentences in statements, questions, and commands;
- distinguish between simple and compound sentences.

Vocabulary

Aries
astrologers
cassette recorder
Gemini
subject (5)
tennis (5)

Teaching Suggestions

1. Discuss the chapter overview and goals with the students.
2. Discuss all vocabulary words and use each in a sentence to ensure understanding.
3. Read all information and examples with the class.
4. Conduct the Warm-Up activities and discuss the correct answers.

Lesson 1. The Subject of the Sentence
Overview

Lesson 1 will help students identify the complete, simple, and compound subjects in sentences. Statements, questions, and commands are also explained.

Lesson Goals

At the conclusion of the lesson, students are expected to:
- identify the complete subject;
- identify the simple subject.

Vocabulary

absent (5)
interrogative
preposition
reverse (6)
snacks (6)

Teaching Suggestions

1. Remind students that adjectives and prepositional phrases are often used to describe nouns and pronouns. The person or thing we are talking about is the subject of a sentence. The simple subject of a sentence is that particular person or thing. The complete subject includes all of the other words that describe the simple subject.
2. Stress that a complete subject may be one word, or it may consist of many words.
3. Conduct each activity and review the correct answers.
4. Do all Follow-Up activities prior to the Lesson Review.

Follow-Up Activities

1. Tell each student to write a subject of a sentence. The subject may be simple or compound and may include adjectives and/or prepositional phrases. The subject may be a noun or pronoun. Collect the papers and read each subject aloud (or students may keep their papers and read them aloud in turn). Ask the students to supply words that will complete the thought to form a complete sentence.
2. Teachers may prepare a list of subjects for conducting the activity described above.
3. Use the sentences in Activities A, B, and C. Each of these sentences is a statement. Write the sentences on the chalkboard or use a transparency and an overhead projector. Ask the students to make the statements into questions. Then, have them identify the subjects in both sentences.
Example:
   Madame Donet teaches French.
Does Madame Donet teach French? (or) Who teaches French?
Ask the students who is being talked about in the sentence.

4. Put these two sentences on the chalkboard and ask the students to explain the difference in meaning:

> Denise shut the door.
> Denise, shut the door.

The first sentence is a statement — the second is a command. The subject of a command is always the person spoken to — the second person pronoun, you. Have each student write a pair of sentences like the example. Put some of them on the chalkboard and discuss.

Lesson 2. The Predicate
Overview
In Lesson 2, students learn to identify the predicate of a simple sentence. Students also practice isolating the verb or verb phrase in a sentence. They learn that portions of the predicate (modifiers and parts of the verb phrase) may appear before the subject. Compound predicates are also explained.

Lesson Goals
At the conclusion of Lesson 2, students are expected to:
- identify the predicate of sentences;
- identify the verb in the predicate.

Vocabulary
adverb	jewelry (5)
apparently (5)	mileage (7)
audience (5)	phrase (5)
earring	preposition
fishing gear (5)	prepositional
include (5)	

Teaching Suggestions
1. Explain that a sentence is a group of words that expresses a complete thought. A complete thought includes identifying who or what we are talking about (subject) and explaining what happened. The second part of the sentence is called the predicate.

   A predicate is a group of words in a sentence that makes a statement about the subject. The predicate includes the verb plus any modifiers (adverbs and prepositional phrases) and other words that complete the idea (objects and complements).

   It is useful at this point to stress that any word that is not part of the subject in a simple sentence is a part of the predicate. Note: conjunctions in compound sentences are not technically part of the complete thought of either sentence.
2. Conduct each activity and discuss all answers.

Follow-Up Activities
1. Ask each student to write one or more predicates on a piece of paper or on the chalkboard. Then, have another student supply a subject for each.
2. Use the sentences in Activities A and B. Tell the students to rewrite the sentences as questions. Then, have them identify the predicate parts of each sentence. For example:
   Brian's best friend, Dennis, moved away.
   Did Brian's best friend, Dennis, move away?
3. Find a reading selection that includes mostly simple or compound sentences. Have students read the sentences aloud and try to identify the predicate. Also, have them identify the verb or verb phrase in each.

Lesson 3. Compound Sentences
Overview
Lesson 3 explains the compound sentence. Students learn to distinguish between a sentence that has a compound subject or a compound predicate and a sentence that has two complete thoughts connected with a conjunction.

Lesson Goals
At the conclusion of the lesson, students are expected to:
- identify the subject and predicate parts of simple and compound sentences;
- identify a compound sentence.

Vocabulary
gerbil	punctuate (7)
hamster	related (7)
mechanic (6)	transportation (5)
motorcycle (6)	

Teaching Suggestions

1. Stress that a compound sentence is two or more complete sentences joined with a conjunction. For example:

   They were hungry, and they were tired.

   Jack was hungry, and Sue was tired.

   Each sentence can stand alone, but the ideas are related in a very close way. The relationship may be time (they occurred together or in a sequence, as in the second example); subject matter (both events happened in the same place). Compound sentences are often used to make comparisons or to point out differences.

2. Remind the student that they must use a comma before the conjunction when they write a compound sentence.

3. Also remind them that a sentence with a compound subject, a compound predicate, or both, is still a simple sentence. For example:

   Carol and her brother went to the beach early in the summer and visited their grandparents in Maine in August.

   Point out the difference between this simple sentence and the following compound sentence:

   Mike likes baseball, and Tom likes soccer.

4. Explain that parts of a compound sentence may be omitted when they are clearly understood. For example:

   Denise has a dog, but Janet does not. (...have a dog.)

Follow-Up Activity

Tell each student to write five sentences with compound subjects, five with compound predicates, five with compound subjects and compound predicates, and five compound sentences. Either the teacher or the students can then read selected sentences aloud, and ask, "Is this a simple sentence or a compound sentence?" Others can identify the type of sentence. Write some of the sentences on the chalkboard and discuss. Identify the subject and the predicate.

Chapter Review

Before assigning the Chapter Review, go over examples of sentences with compound subjects and compound predicates. Also, review statements, questions, and commands. Review all of the vocabulary, including the words *helmet* (5) and *prefer* (6) that appear in the review exercises.

Review Activities

1. The topic of horoscopes, astrology, and the zodiac appear in some of the chapter activities. Students may enjoy reading about their own signs and writing brief descriptions of what people with those signs are supposed to be like. These descriptions may be written as paragraphs or as lists of sentences. Then, have students read their descriptions aloud. Others can identify the sentences as either simple or compound. Sentences can also be identified according to purpose — statement, question, or imperative; or they may be divided into the subject and predicate parts.

2. In Chapter 10, Andy finally decides to buy a motorcycle, although he has been looking at cars throughout previous activities. Students may write sentences comparing cars and motorcycles. Many of these sentences should be compound. They may also contain compound subjects and predicates. These sentences should be analyzed to determine subject and predicate parts, purpose, and structure (simple or compound).

Answer Key to Chapter 10
Warm-Up A
1. Mary
2. Her birthday
3. she
4. Her mother
5. you
6. you (understood)
7. April third

Warm-Up B
1. know about their "sun sign"
2. write daily horoscopes for the newspaper
3. is an Aries
4. was also born under that sign
5. is a ram
6. likes to be independent
7. will probably open her own doors

Warm-Up C
1. compound subject
2. compound sentence
3. compound predicate

Lesson 1, pages 199-203
Activity A
1. Madame Donet
2. The entire class
3. The teacher
4. They
5. The students in the class

Activity B
1. Each 4. All
2. All 5. Two
3. eight

Activity C
1. I
2. Kim and Stephanie
3. Three of our classmates
4. One of my friends
5. Everyone in the band

Activity D
1. program 4. school
2. bus stop 5. books
3. answer

Activity E
1. meeting 4. you
2. time 5. group
3. What

Activity F
1. Bruce 4. you (understood)
2. you (understood) 5. you (understood)
3. you (understood)

Activity G
1. Fred, Alice 4. you (understood)
2. hat, gloves 5. books, papers
3. spring, summer 6. sodas, snacks

Lesson Review
1. baseball season
2. James
3. He
4. a try-out
5. Bruce and Andy
6. The college
7. Most of last year's team
8. the try-outs

Lesson 2, pages 204-208
Activity A
1. was lost yesterday
2. looked everywhere for it
3. found it today
4. was missing
5. apparently stepped on it
6. walked home with Denise
7. greeted them with loud barks
8. tried to cheer up Brenda
9. had been her favorite jewelry

Activity B
1. gave Mary a surprise birthday party
2. baked the cake
3. drove Mary to band practice that day
4. came over and decorated the house
5. came home about six-thirty
6. jumped out
7. screamed "Surprise!"
8. was delicious
9. ate two pieces
10. was very pleased about that

Activity C

1. (Did). . .(bring)Sheba to the party

2. Why(was). . .(left)at home

3. Maybe . . .(didn't have)a present

4. After the party . . .(wrapped)up a piece of cake to take home

5. (Was). . . for Sheba

6. (is)only a cat

7. (can't)really(expect)a piece of cake

8. At eleven-thirty . . .(heard)Denise's key in the door

9. Usually . . .(meows)happily

10. Tonight . . .(was)unusually quiet

11. Then . . .(saw)the cake in Denise's hand

12. In an instant . . .(was meowing)happily

Activity D

1. (looked)at new cars but(didn't buy)one

2. (cost)too much and(used)too much gas

3. (got)good gas mileage but(were)also expensive

4. (were)often rusty and(needed)repairs

5. (thought and thought)but(couldn't make)a decision

Activity E
Answers will vary.

Activity F
1. Do like
2. wanted
3. do like
4. likes
5. likes

Lesson Review

1. In the spring . . .(gets)warm

2. (think)about outdoor activities

3. (are planting)flowers

4. (gets)his fishing gear out

5. always(know)the first day of spring

6. (is)out in his yard with his fishing rod

7. (likes)to practice casting

8. This year . . .(plans)to catch a huge fish

9. (wants)to catch the big one

10. Last year . . .(got)away

11. (will)be different

12. (has)already(invited)us to the fish fry

Lesson 3, pages 209-211
Activity A, (the predicate is in bold print)
1. After the party they **were hungry;** however, all of the restaurants **were closed.**

2. Alice **has a cat,** Mike **has a gerbil,** and Sandy **has a hamster.**

3. Mr. Barry **likes sweets,** but Mrs. Barry **prefers fruit.**

4. Andy **wants to be a catcher,** but Bruce **likes to play third base.**

5. The new French teacher **gives a lot of homework,** but his tests **are usually easy.**

Activity B
Answers will vary.

Activity C
1. No
2. Yes
3. No
4. Yes
5. No

Lesson Review (the predicate is in bold print)
1. <u>Andy</u> **counted his money and made a decision.** - No

2. <u>Most of the cars in town</u> **were too expensive,** but <u>one form of transportation</u> **was just right.** - Yes

3. <u>He</u> **needed something to drive to work,** and <u>he</u> **also needed something to drive to school.** - Yes

4. <u>Bruce and Andy</u> **went to the showroom.** - No

5. <u>Andy's new wheels</u> **were there,** and <u>they</u> **looked great.** - Yes

6. <u>The motorcycle</u> **was not a fancy car,** but <u>Andy</u> **was happy!** - Yes

Chapter Review (the predicate is in bold print)
Part A
1. <u>Everyone</u> **liked Andy's new motorcycle.**

2. <u>Denise and Mary</u> **wanted a ride.**

3. <u>Andy</u> **gave Denise a crash helmet.**

4. <u>She</u> **hopped on the back and smiled.**

5. "**Have** <u>you</u> **ever ridden on a bike before?**"

6. <u>She</u> **shook her head.**

7. "**Then** <u>this ride</u> **will be especially fun.**"

8. <u>There</u> **was a small breeze that day.**

9. <u>They</u> **rode around the block and returned.**

10. "(<u>You</u>) **Give me a turn!**"

Part B
1. <u>The motorcycle</u> **took off,** and <u>Corey</u> **screamed.** - Yes

2. "<u>It</u> **is going too fast for me!**" - No

3. <u>Corey</u> **held on tightly,** but <u>he</u> **was still afraid.** - Yes

4. <u>Denise and Bruce</u> **stood on the curb and waited for Andy and Corey.** - No

5. **In a few minutes** <u>Andy</u> **pulled up,** and <u>Corey</u> **got off.** - Yes

6. "<u>That</u> **was fun,** but <u>I</u> **prefer a car.**" - Yes

7. <u>Corey</u> **bent down and kissed the ground.** - No

8. <u>Bruce</u> **just shook his head.** - No

Chapter 11
Sentence Patterns

Overview

Chapter 11 has four lessons. Lesson 1 presents Pattern 1 sentences and intransitive verbs. The remaining three sentence patterns introduced in this chapter require transitive verbs. Pattern 2 sentences contain direct objects; Pattern 3 sentences add an indirect object; and Pattern 4 sentences contain an objective complement. In each lesson, students learn to expand sentences with modifiers or compounds. They also identify patterns in sentences that make statements, ask questions, or issue commands.

Chapter Goals

At the conclusion of Chapter 11, students are expected to:
* distinguish between transitive and intransitive verbs;
* identify four sentence patterns;
* diagram four sentence patterns.

Vocabulary

basic (7)	motorcycle (6)
director (7)	predicate
identify (6)	solo (6)
intransitive	transitive

Teaching Suggestions

1. A pattern is a special way that something is arranged. It can be a guide or a model that is repeated many times. In English (and in all languages), words are arranged in special ways to express ideas. It is important for students to understand these patterns are descriptive.
2. Explain the difference between a transitive and an intransitive verb. Some actions cannot be performed without another person or thing to receive the action. The action is transferred to the other person or thing.
   For example:
   Andy bought is not a complete idea. If someone said those words, we would wonder "bought what?" *Buy* is an instance of an action that cannot be completed without another thing. The action is transitive. It must be transferred to something.

Lesson 1. Pattern 1 Sentences
Overview

Lesson 1 develops the concept of an intransitive action and helps the students recognize Pattern 1 sentences. Students also learn to expand sentences by adding adverbs and prepositional phrases. Questions and compound sentences are explained. Students are introduced to diagraming as an aid to understanding sentence structure.

Lesson Goals

At the conclusion of this lesson, students are expected to:
* identify the complete subject of a Pattern 1 sentence;
* identify the complete predicate of a Pattern 1 sentence.

Vocabulary

adverb	expand (6)
audience (5)	horizontal (7)
basic (7)	intransitive
column (5)	predicate
compound (6)	prepositional
diagram (6)	vertical (6)

Teaching Suggestions

1. Explain that the Pattern 1 sentence is the simplest kind of sentence and is used only to express very simple, uncomplicated ideas.
2. The verb *to be* is a special case. *Be* as a main verb is always intransitive. In Chapter 12, students will study sentence patterns in which *be* is a linking verb. *Be* is also used in a special type of Pattern 1 sentence in which the complement is an adverb or a prepositional phrase. For example:
   He *is* there.
   He *is* home. (Home is an adverbial noun.)
   He *is* in his room.
   Students should understand that while intransitive verbs usually do not require additional words in order to express a complete idea, there are exceptions.

Follow-Up Activity

If the students continue to have difficulty with the concept of intransitive, have them act out verbs such as : hit, laugh, walk, skip, jump, leave, read, paint, choose, give, and kneel. In order to act out the transitive verbs, they will need to use another person or object to complete the action. If the verb is intransitive, they will be able to do the action without the involvement of an additional person or object.

Lesson 2. Pattern 2 Sentences
Overview

In Lesson 2, students deal with Pattern 2 sentences, which have a transitive verb and a direct object. The direct object is required to express the complete thought in these sentences. The objective form of the pronoun is reviewed. Students practice with statements, questions, commands, and compound forms. In the diagraming exercises, students are introduced to sentences in which the subject is understood.

Lesson Goals

At the conclusion of this lesson, students are expected to:
* locate the direct object in sentences;
* distinguish between Pattern 1 and Pattern 2 sentences (intransitive and transitive verbs).

Vocabulary

compound (6)	secretary (5)
condominium	tense (6)
home economics	transitive
icing	vanilla (6)
request (6)	vertical (6)

Teaching Suggestions

1. Explain that a Pattern 2 sentence has a subject and a predicate, and that the predicate must have a verb and a direct object. The direct object is either a noun or pronoun. It receives the action to complete the idea and form a sentence.
2. Tell the students that to find the direct object, they should say the verb and then ask the question what? or whom?

Lesson 3. Pattern 3 Sentences
Overview

In Lesson 3, Sentence Pattern 3 and indirect objects are introduced. Students learn to expand those sentences by compounding or by using modifiers. The diagraming practice shows how to illustrate compound parts of a sentence.

Lesson Goals

At the conclusion of Lesson 3, students are expected to:
* identify the indirect object in a sentence;
* distinguish between Patterns 1, 2, and 3.

Vocabulary

Academy (5)	indirect
award (5)	Oscar
column (5)	rearrange
compound (6)	title (5)
expand (6)	

Teaching Suggestion

Point out that the indirect object is a noun or pronoun that occurs before the direct object in a sentence. In most cases, the indirect object can be changed to a prepositional phrase and placed after the direct object. Grammatically, the second construction is considered to be a prepositional phrase. In a diagram, both constructions would look the same except that the preposition would be missing in the case of an indirect object. The preposition will be either *to* or *for*.

Lesson 4. Pattern 4 Sentences
Overview

Pattern 4 sentences are presented in this lesson. The objective complement is also introduced.

Lesson Goal

At the conclusion of this lesson, students are expected to identify the objective complement in a sentence.

Vocabulary

complement (10)	elect (5)
compliment (5)	spicy (5)
dye (5)	

Teaching Suggestions

1. Explain the difference between the words *compliment* and *complement*. Stress that the objective complement refers back to the direct object and not to the verb. The objective complement, if it is an adjective, describes the object. If it is a noun, it renames the object. It is, therefore, another word with the same or a similar meaning.

2. When diagraming Pattern 4 sentences, remember that the objective complement is necessary to complete the idea expressed in the sentence, therefore, it is placed on the base line of the sentence diagram.

Chapter Review

Before beginning the Chapter Review exercises, conduct some of the review activities below. Also, conduct any Follow-Up activities that were previously omitted.

Vocabulary

attach (5)	recipe
computer (8)	video
microcomputer	

Review Activity

Be sure that students can distinguish between intransitive and transitive verbs. Choose an interesting topic and have students write simple sentences that represent Patterns 1, 2, 3, and 4. Write model sentences on the chalkboard.

Answer Key to Chapter 11
Warm-Up

1.	Pattern 3	3.	Pattern 4
2.	Pattern 2	4.	Pattern 1
5.	Pattern 1	7.	Pattern 3
6.	Pattern 2	8.	Pattern 4

Lesson 1, pages 215-222
Activity A

1. band / was
2. audience / clapped
3. Donna / laughed
4. kitten / purred
5. She / has
6. They / were
7. I / am
8. friend / moved
9. block / are
10. Dinner / is

Activity B

	Verb	Adverb
1.	is burning	brightly
2.	can run	fast
3.	is smiling	usually
4.	practices	often
5.	am reading	now
6.	is walking	rapidly
7.	rained	Yesterday

Activity C
Answers will vary.

Activity D

1. Everyone (laughs) at Tiny.

2. Karl (is leaving) for school.

3. Our neighbors (moved) to Ohio.

4. Mr. Nelson (works) at the post office.

5. The book (fell) off the shelf.

Activity E
Answers will vary.

Activity F

1.	Will leave	4.	Is practicing
2.	fell	5.	Are listening
3.	does work		

Activity G

1.	Yes	6.	Yes
2.	Yes	7.	Yes
3.	No	8.	No
4.	Yes	9.	No
5.	No	10.	No

Activity H

A. Complete subjects
1. The book and the pencil
2. Alison

3. Alison and the band
4. Alison and Frank . . . they
5. Clarissa . . . she

B. Simple subjects
1. book / pencil
2. Alison
3. Alison / band
4. Alison / Frank . . . they
5. Clarissa . . . she

C. Complete predicates
1. fell on the floor
2. laughed first and then cried
3. are thinking about their trip and talking to each other
4. were on time . . . had to run down the hall
5. was reading in the morning . . . was writing in the afternoon

D. Verb or verb phrases
1. fell
2. laughed / cried
3. are thinking / talking
4. were / had
5. was reading / was writing

Activity I
Answers will vary.

Activity J
1. The band played.
2. Mrs. Nelson left.
3. Everyone laughed
4. Which student reported?
5. Is Tiny barking?
6. Several cried.
7. Emilio's motorcycle rides.
8. He inquired.
9. Are you leaving?
10. Alison's band will go and play.

Activity K
1.

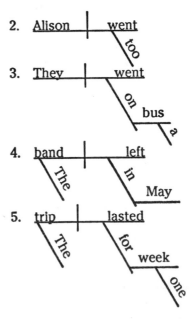

Lesson Review (predicate is in bold print)
1. <u>Which students</u> **are in the band room?**
2. <u>Everyone</u> **will ride on the bus.**
3. <u>Alison's trumpet</u> **fell on the floor.**
4. **Luckily** <u>it</u> **did not break.**
5. <u>Alison</u> **almost cried!**
6. <u>Alison</u> **is ready for the trip.**
7. <u>Everyone in the band</u> **is thinking about the trip.**
8. <u>Sue and Rita</u> **are not going.**
9. <u>They</u> **will stay in school.**
10. <u>The band</u> **has been practicing and preparing for the trip for a long time.**

Lesson 2, pages 223-231
Activity A
1. verbs
2. them
3. objects
4. them
5. hand
6. answers

Activity B
Answers will vary.
Suggested responses are:
1. a car; a coat
2. a movie
3. chicken; steak
4. some ice cream
5. French; music
6. his bone; his way

Activity C
1. I
2. him
3. him
4. them
5. She
6. We

Activity D

Subject   Verb   Object
1. Sam / received / a letter.
2. The tabby cat / caught / a mouse.
3. I / have been studying / French.
4. The firefighters / were climbing / the ladders.
5. Mr. Nelson / loves / that old song!
6. We / cannot find / her.

Activity E

1. bought his tickets early
2. can diagram this sentence
3. eats his dinner rapidly
4. can easily find the subject
5. Yesterday, lost his notebook
6. found it today

Activity F

1. wrote a letter (to her Uncle Albert)
2. painted their house (with bright colors)
3. wanted a new food dish (for his birthday)
4. filled the fish tank (to the top)
5. made pancakes (for breakfast)
6. found some blue shoes (with white trim)

Activity G

Answers will vary.

Activity H

1. typed
2. Is typing
3. Have fished
4. is typing
5. Can type
6. Has seen

Activity I

1. (Take) book
2. (Make) cake
3. (Finish) work
4. (Hang) coat
5. (Have) piece
6. (Read) sentences

Activity J

Answers will vary.

Activity K

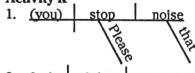

1. (you) | stop | noise / Please / that

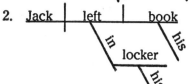

2. Jack | left | book / in / locker / his / his

3. you | Have seen | Sally

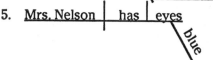

4. Rita | likes | poetry / by / Edgar Allan Poe

5. Mrs. Nelson | has | eyes / blue

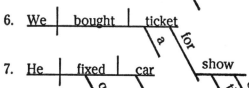

6. We | bought | ticket / a / for / show / the / early

7. He | fixed | car / quickly / the

Lesson Review
Part A

1. questions
2. questions
3. Sue
4. Rita / Alison
5. movie
6. book
7. it
8. story

Part B

1. Pattern 1
2. Pattern 2
3. Pattern 2
4. Pattern 1
5. Pattern 2
6. Pattern 1

Lesson 3, pages 232-241
Activity A
1. her mother
2. Alison
3. Jim
4. her
5. Sue
6. Tim
7. Mr. Nelson
8. Alison
9. himself
10. Tim

Activity B
1. Rita gave a bone to Tiny.
2. Mrs. Nelson paid twenty dollars to the grocer.
3. Emilio lent his motorcycle to Tim.
4. Sue asked a question to Alison.
5. The waitress served lunch to Sue and Alison.
6. Mother bought a gift for Tim.

Activity C
1. The teacher found Alison a book.
2. Tim bought himself a new coat.
3. Sue handed Rita the note.
4. Alison fixed herself lunch.
5. The university gave the student a diploma.

Activity D
1. The director / gave / the band / their music.
2. Fred / asked / Mr. Smith / a question.
3. The music company / sent / the school / a bill.
4. Mr. Smith / handed / Alison / her trumpet.
5. Mr. Smith / offered / the students / his help.
6. The teacher / gave / the class / homework.
7. Sue / taught / Rita / sign language.
8. Alison / wrote / her aunt / a letter.
9. The school / awarded / Tim / a scholarship.
10. Mr. Jackson / gave / Tim / a raise.

Activity E
1. Sue told me a secret.
2. Tim made Alison a cake.
3. The waitress served them dinner.
4. Rita wrote her aunt a letter.
5. Emilio gave Tiny a bath.
6. The coach told the team the play.
7. Rita bought Tiny a ribbon.
8. Alison fixed herself a snack.
9. Alison lent me her sweater.
10. He handed him a dollar.

Activity F
1. I
2. him
3. her
4. us
5. We
6. them

Activity G
Answers will vary. Suggested responses are:
1. her best friend
   her friend from school
2. the old lady
   the lady on the bus
3. the young boy
   the boy in the front row
4. our next-door neighbor
   our neighbor on the corner
5. the two people
   the two people in the red house

Activity H
1. Rita
2. me
3. Alison
4. Alison
5. Christopher Columbus

Activity I
1. me
2. me
3. us
4. me
5. yourself

Activity J
Answers will vary.

Activity K
1. Pattern 2
2. Pattern 3
3. Pattern 2
4. Pattern 2
5. Pattern 3
6. Pattern 2
7. Pattern 2
8. Pattern 3
9. Pattern 2
10. Pattern 3

Activity L
1. (you) | pass | bread
   Please / me / the
2. Jack | lent | car
   Larry / his

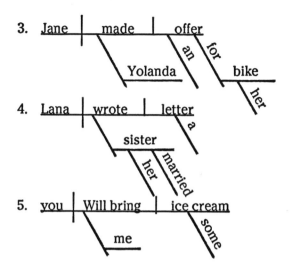

3. Jane | made | offer
an / for bike
Yolanda / her

4. Lana | wrote | letter
sister / a
her / married / some

5. you | Will bring | ice cream
me

2. classmates | elected | Jack \ treasurer
His

3. She | made | pie \ spicy
the

4. They | named | Mrs. Nelson \ Woman
of
Year
the

5. Alison | painted | room \ yellow
her

Lesson Review
Part A
1. Rita (and) Pam
2. (the) family
3. (his) grandfather
4. me
5. yourself

Part B
1. Pattern 2
2. Pattern 3
3. Pattern 2
4. Pattern 1
5. Pattern 3

Lesson 4, pages 242-244
Activity A
1. president
2. (many) colors
3. beautiful
4. dead
5. sleepy
6. (a great) actor
7. president
8. beautiful
9. sweet
10. brown

Activity B
Answers will vary. Suggested responses are:
1. interesting
2. beautiful
3. treasurer
4. hot
5. Charles

Activity C
Correct answers will vary.

Activity D
1. Emilio | found | class \ interesting
his / computer

Lesson Review
1. (the) winner
2. (our) leader
3. silver
4. (many) colors
5. (too) fattening

Chapter Review
Part A
1. transitive (computer)
2. transitive (it)
3. intransitive
4. transitive (computer)
5. intransitive
6. transitive (it)
7. transitive (video games)
8. transitive (recipe file)
9. transitive (it)
10. intransitive

Part B
1. Pattern 2
2. Pattern 1
3. Pattern 3
4. Pattern 3
5. Pattern 4

Part C
1. We | can do | math
on / our
microcomputer
the

2. It | can add
fast

3.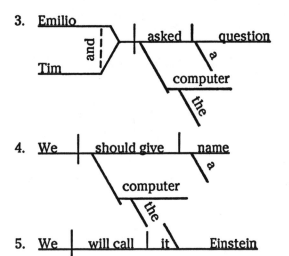

4. We | should give | name
         computer
              the
       a

5. We | will call | it \ Einstein

Chapter 12
Sentence Patterns with a Linking Verb

Overview

Chapter 12 presents the two sentence patterns that contain linking verbs. Lesson 1 explains the predicate adjective, and Lesson 2 explains predicate nouns and pronouns.

Chapter Goals

At the conclusion of Chapter 12, students are expected to:
- identify linking verbs in sentences;
- distinguish between predicate adjectives and predicate nouns or pronouns.

Vocabulary

active (6)   intransitive   predicate

Teaching Suggestions

1. Review the differences between action and state-of-being verbs. Then, remind students that an action verb can be transitive or intransitive, but a state-of-being verb is always intransitive. It expresses no action; therefore, it can never transfer action to an object.
2. Students should understand that the differences among the sentence patterns are always associated with the predicate part of the sentence and particularly related to the verb. The verb is the crucial word in our language as we seek to express our ideas.

Lesson 1. Pattern 5 Sentences
Overview

Lesson 1 introduces Sentence Pattern 5, which includes a subject, a linking verb, and an adjective. It develops the concept that the linking verb and the adjective are both necessary to express the complete idea. Imperative sentences, questions, and compound sentences are explained. Students are taught to expand the sentence by adding modifiers. Diagraming is also included.

Lesson Goals

At the conclusion of the lesson, students are expected to:
- identify the linking verb in a sentence;
- identify the predicate adjective in a sentence;

- distinguish between linking verbs and non-linking verbs.

Vocabulary

athletic (5)	connected (5)	extremely (6)
artistic	cube (6)	frisky (6)
column (5)	describe (5)	microcomputer
request (6)	relaxed (5)	spry (7)

Teaching Suggestion

Discuss the introductory information and examples. Conduct these activities orally so that students become familiar with the "sound" of this sentence pattern. In speaking, some students may omit the verb, *be*. Teachers should point out that the idea may be conveyed when the verb *be* is omitted, but that correct usage requires the presence of the linking verb.

Lesson 2. Pattern 6 Sentences
Overview

In Lesson 2, the final sentence pattern is presented: subject, linking verb, noun (or pronoun). Imperative sentences, questions, and compound structure are presented. Included in diagraming practice are compound sentences and questions.

Lesson Goals

At the conclusion of Lesson 2, student are expected to:
- identify the linking verb in sentences;
- identify the key words in the sentence pattern (subject, linking verb, and noun or pronoun).

Vocabulary

author (6)	finch	musical (5)
beverage (8)	label (6)	novelist
capital (5)	lawyer (5)	spicy (5)
comedies (7)	motorcyclist	wren (6)

Teaching Suggestions

1. Stress that if there is a predicate pronoun, this pronoun will be in the nominative case. It refers back to the subject or renames it.
2. Point out that the predicate noun may be described by adjectives. Those adjectives ap-

pear in the predicate, but they describe the predicate noun — not the subject.

3. The direct object and the predicate noun both appear in the same location in a sentence — directly after the verb. Activity C should be discussed thoroughly.

Follow-Up Activity

Prepare a list of Pattern 5 and Pattern 6 sentences. Use only the basic words (omit prepositional phrases). Then, scramble the words. Have the students arrange the words in sentences.
For example:
1. A cheerleader Beth became.
2. Jimmy athlete is.
3. Good we are friends.

Chapter Review

Before beginning the Chapter Review exercises, discuss the difference between an active transitive verb with a direct object and a linking verb. Be sure students know that a predicate noun or predicate adjective refers back to the subject. Conduct the Follow-Up exercises for Lessons 1 and 2 that may have been omitted previously, or use one of the suggested review activities below.

Review Activities

1. Divide the class into six groups and assign a sentence pattern to each group. Students should develop five sentences in the assigned pattern. Each group should then be asked to present the pattern and diagram sample sentences for the other students in the class.
2. Select a brief short story or essay from a literature book or magazine. Read each sentence aloud. Ask the students to identify the part of the sentence and name the pattern for each.

Answer Key for Chapter 12
Warm-Up A
1.	Action	4.	Linking
2.	Action	5.	Action
3.	Linking	6.	Linking

Warm-Up B
1.	keeps	4.	is

2. is   5. is
3. are

Warm-Up C
1.	friendly	4.	friends
2.	shy	5.	senior
3.	student		

Lesson 1, pages 249-257
Activity A
Answers will vary.

Activity B
Answers will vary.

Activity C
1. New - cars
   expensive - cars
2. That - boy
   little - boy
   hungry - boy
3. My - brother
   youngest - brother
   taller - brother
   taller - brother
4. The - cake
   birthday - cake
   chocolate - cake
5. warm - Tomorrow
   sunny - Tomorrow

Activity D
Subject   Linking Verb   Adjective
1. The sunset / was / lovely.
2. My cousin / is / artistic.
3. The state of Florida / is / warm.
4. Rubik's cube / is / colorful.
5. The apartment / is / large.

Activity E
Answers will vary.

Activity F
Answers will vary.

Activity G
1. June / is / pleasant
2. days / grow / longer
3. air / feels / warmer

4. Maryanne / is / happy
5. Tiny / becomes / friskier

Activity H
Answers will vary.

Activity I
1. Look friendly
2. Be nice
3. Be careful
4. Be ready
5. Remain loyal and true

Activity J

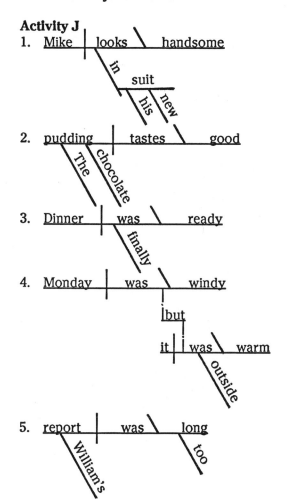

1. Mike | looks \ handsome
   in suit his new
2. pudding | tastes \ good
   The chocolate
3. Dinner | was \ ready
   finally
4. Monday | was \ windy
   but
   it | was \ warm
   outside
5. report | was \ long
   William's too

Lesson Review
Part A
1. tasted   3. is
2. appears   4. has been

Part B
1. small / powerful   4. careful
2. chilly   5. long
3. good

Part C
1. Yes
2. No
3. No
4. Yes
5. Yes

Lesson 2, pages 258-263
Activity A
Answers 1, 2, and 4 will vary.
3. Mt. Everest
5. Paris

Activity B
1. president   4. Ted
2. cook   5. He
3. Carol

Activity C
1. direct object   4. direct object
2. predicate noun 5. predicate noun
3. predicate noun

Activity D
1. country   5. movie
2. one   6. *Star Wars*
3. planet   7. friend
4. beverage

Activity E
Answers will vary.

Activity F
   Subject   Linking Verb   Predicate Noun
1. Franklin Pierce / was / president
2. trees / are / oaks, maples
3. bird / is / wren, finch

4. Maryanne / has been / student
5. *The Good Earth* / is / movie, book
6. Ted / is student, salesclerk

Activity G

1. 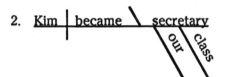 Who | is \ she   or   she | is \ Who

2. 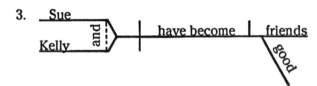 Kim | became \ secretary / our / class

3. 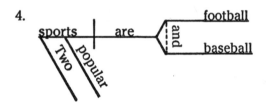 Sue and Kelly | have become | friends \ good

4. 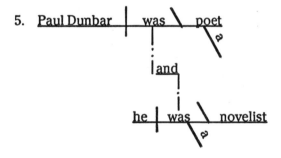 sports | are \ football and baseball / Two / popular

5. Paul Dunbar | was \ poet / a
   ⋮ and
   he | was \ novelist / a

Lesson Review

Part A

1. is
2. was
3. is
4. Was
5. has been

Part B

1. desserts - subject
   are - linking verb
   pie and cake - predicate nouns
2. weather - subject
   feels - linking verb
   chilly - adjective
3. (You) - subject
   be - linking verb
   true - adjective
4. Jupiter - subject
   is - linking verb
   planet - predicate noun
5. lake - subject
   is - linking verb
   quiet and peaceful - adjective
6. Don - subject
   Is - linking verb
   friend - predicate noun
7. Who - subject
   was - linking verb
   that - predicate noun
8. Lima - subject
   is - linking verb
   capital - predicate noun

Chapter Review

Part A

1. Taste - No
2. is - Yes
3. tastes - Yes
4. Are - Yes
5. have eaten - No
6. am - Yes
7. fixed - No
8. am - Yes
9. want - No
10. will eat - No

Part B

1. predicate adjective
2. predicate noun
3. predicate noun
4. predicate noun
5. predicate noun
6. predicate noun
7. predicate pronoun
8. predicate pronoun
9. predicate adjective
10. predicate noun

Chapter 13
Complex Sentences

Overview

Chapter 13 introduces the complex and compound-complex sentences. Lessons 1 through 3 deal with the adverb, noun, and adjective clauses, respectively. The final lesson presents the compound-complex sentence and provides practice in analyzing the structure of sentences.

Chapter Goals

At the conclusion of this chapter, students are expected to:
- distinguish between phrases and clauses;
- locate dependent clauses in sentences and identify their function (adverb, noun, or adjective);
- locate the independent and dependent clauses in compound and complex sentences and identify the sentence patterns of each clause;
- distinguish among simple, compound, complex, and compound-complex sentences.

Vocabulary

clause (7)	independent (6)
complex (9)	phrase (6)
compound (6)	predicate
constructed	relative (5)
dependent (7)	structure (6)
describe (5)	subject (5)
identify (6)	subordinating

Teaching Suggestions
1. Review the vocabulary words and point them out as they are encountered in the Warm-Up activities. The only new term is *structure*, meaning framework organization, plan, arrangement, or design. Structure refers to the complexity of the sentence rather than to the components of the sentence or pattern. Sentences are either simple, compound, complex, or compound-complex. Be sure students understand that a sentence with a compound element such as a compound subject is still a simple sentence.
2. Be sure that students understand that a clause must have a subject and a predicate (verb). A phrase may have a subject, it may have a verb, or it may have neither a subject nor a verb. A phrase is any group of related words. A noun with its adjectives is a phrase.
3. Remind students that sentences can be grouped according to purpose, pattern, or structure.

Follow-Up Activity

Conduct additional drills if students are unable to distinguish between phrases and clauses. Use any paragraph from a literature book, a magazine, or a newspaper. Have the students find subjects, predicates, prepositional phrases, and verb phrases. Then, have the students find clauses — groups of words with a subject and a verb.

Lesson 1. The Adverb Clause
Overview

Lesson 1 presents the adverb clause. Adverb clauses that modify verbs, adjectives, and other adverbs are included. Incomplete clauses are explained.

Lesson Goals

At the conclusion of Lesson 1, students are expected to:
- identify dependent adverb clauses in sentences;
- locate the subject and verb in each clause;
- distinguish between independent and dependent clauses;
- distinguish between simple and complex sentences.

Vocabulary

adverb	label (6)
deaf (5)	parentheses
incomplete (7)	transportation (5)

Teaching Suggestions
1. Review the objectives and the new vocabulary words.
2. Be sure students know that when a word or group of words answers a question about the verb, it is an adverb. Also, remind them that adverbs of degree answer questions about adjectives and other adverbs.

3. As you go through this lesson, ask students to point out the sentence patterns in independent clauses. Also, ask them what question the adverb clause is answering.

4. On page 271, students learn that certain words in an adverb of degree clause are usually omitted. We say that they are understood because the listener or reader knows or understands that they are part of the complete thought. We say, for example "She is taller than her sister." We know or understand that the entire clause is "than her sister is tall."

Follow-Up Activity

Divide the class into three groups. Group 1 should write several adverb clauses that answer the question why? Group 2 should be assigned *when?* and Group 3, *where?* The teacher writes several simple sentences that make a statement using an action verb. Then, proceed as follows: Teacher: (Read a sentence.) Does anyone have a clause that tells us *why, when,* or *where* this happened?

Write the sentence with the appropriate adverb clause or clauses on the board. Continue until all of the sentences and clauses are used.

Lesson 2. The Noun Clause
Overview

Lesson 2 explains the noun clause as it is used as a subject, predicate noun, direct object, object of the preposition, and appositive. Different forms of the pronoun *who* are explained. The omission of the relative pronoun *that* is also discussed.

Lesson Goals

At the conclusion of this lesson, students are expected to:
- locate noun clauses in sentences;
- identify the function of noun clauses in selected sentences.

Vocabulary

amendment (7)	relative (5)
appositive	revolve (6)
bibliography (9)	scientific (6)
constitutional (6)	

Teaching Suggestions

1. Go over the new vocabulary words and discuss the lesson objectives.

2. The relative pronoun with its function in the noun clause is presented on pages 274-275. The difficult part of this concept is that the pronoun, if it is used as an object, will be placed before the subject of the clause. Stress that the relative pronoun introduces the noun clause and so it must come first, even though its part (function) in the pattern may be as the direct object. The same logic is operating for the predicate noun placement.

3. On page 275, students learn that the relative pronoun tha*t* may be omitted. A noun clause is more difficult to locate when *that* is omitted. Whether to include *that* in a sentence is a matter of personal choice.

4. Tell the students that while adverb clauses can usually be omitted from a sentence, noun clauses usually cannot be omitted. We cannot omit the subject, the direct object, the predicate noun, or the object of a preposition from a sentence pattern; however, sometimes an appositive may be omitted.

Follow-Up Activity

Divide the class into two teams. Tell each team to write at least two sentences with noun clauses used as: subjects, predicate nouns, direct objects, objects of the preposition, and appositives. The total number of sentences produced by both groups should equal the number of students in the class.

Have a member of Team 1 read a sentence aloud. A member of Team 2 will try to identify the noun clause and tell its function in the sentence. If successful, the team gets a point. Alternate until every member of the class has read a sentence and identified the noun clause and its function. Sentences that are missed should be written on the chalkboard.

Do this activity over a two-day period to give the teacher time to collect and check the sentences.

Lesson 3. The Adjective Clause
Overview
Lesson 3 explains the adjective clause. The pronoun that may be omitted in the case of relative pronouns introducing noun clauses.

Lesson Goals
At the conclusion of this lesson, students are expected to:
- identify adjective clauses in sentences;
- identify the noun or pronoun that the adjective clause is describing;
- distinguish among simple, compound, and complex sentences.

Vocabulary
absent (5)   organize (6)   guarantee (7)

Teaching Suggestion
Review the function of an adjective in a sentence. An adjective in a sentence usually is placed before the noun it modifies, but it may also follow a linking verb. Adjective phrases and clauses however, are placed after the noun or pronoun they describe. Placement in another location in the sentence results in a "dangling adjective clause" and a grammatically poor sentence.

Follow-Up Activity
Select a passage in a literature book, magazine, or newspaper. Tell the students to locate each relative pronoun and the clause that follows. Then, decide whether the clause is an adjective or a noun. If an adjective, what noun or pronoun is it describing? If a noun, what is its function in the sentence? Tell the students to also look for clauses that are not introduced by a relative pronoun because the word *that* has been omitted.

Lesson 4. Complex and Compound-Complex Sentences
Overview
In Lesson 4, students analyze sentences to determine whether they are compound, complex, or compound-complex. Students learn that a sentence can have more than one dependent clause and that the same idea can be expressed in several ways.

Lesson Goal
At the conclusion of the lesson, students are expected to distinguish among simple, compound, complex, and compound-complex sentences.

Vocabulary
analyze (8)	golf (5)
college (5)	graduate (6)
conquer (5)	plantation (5)
decision (5)	putter
diagram (6)	scholarship (5)
discouraged (6)	transitive
errand (5)	

Teaching Suggestions
1. Discuss the new vocabulary words and the lesson objectives with the students.
2. Tell the students that the compound-complex sentence is simply a compound sentence with one or more dependent clauses. Students must locate the independent clause to determine the structure of a sentence.
3. Explain that the students have been analyzing sentences throughout Part 2 of this text. They have analyzed sentences to determine sentence patterns. Now, they are analyzing to determine the structure of those sentences — simple, compound, complex, compound-complex.
4. Page 283 mentions Richard Wright, a black American writer, who was born in 1908 and died in 1960. His first novel, *Native Son*, published in 1940, was very successful. It was later adapted for the stage and the movie screen. His work is widely read today. Students may wish to read his work or a biography of Wright.
5. On page 286, the structure of sentences with direct and indirect quotations is explained. Students can analyze the pattern and the structure of the quotation itself; however, the quotation is also structurally an object of a verb. Jackie said, "Let's go." The quotation answers the question *what?* and receives the action of the verb.

Follow-Up Activity
Select a story with dialog. Have the students analyze each sentence, including the direct quota-

tions. They should be able to identify any sentence as either simple, compound, complex, or compound-complex and to analyze the pattern of each clause, independent or dependent.

Chapter Review

Before beginning the Chapter Review, conduct any Follow-Up activities previously omitted. If students have mastered the objectives of this chapter, they should make no more than one error in each part of the review.

Review Activities

1. Have students write several sentences about an assigned topic. Have them skip lines between sentences so that they can identify the structure of each sentence — simple, compound, complex, or compound-complex. Tell them to write at least one sentence for each of those structures.
2. Go back to the early chapters of this text at random. Select activities and ask the students to identify the subject and the verb in each clause in each sentence. Have them identify the complex sentences.

Answer Key to Chapter 13
Warm-Up A
1. Phrase
2. Clause
3. Phrase
4. Phrase
5. Clause

Warm-Up B
1. who just joined the team
2. who won the contest
3. until she finishes
4. Before the game began
5. whoever finished first

Warm-Up C
1. Because
2. if
3. that
4. who
5. What

Warm-Up D
1. Shelly - subject
   missed - verb
   bus - direct object

2. Rick - subject
   will hit - verb
   run - direct object
3. (You) - subject
   paint - verb
   house - direct object
   green - object complement

Warm-Up E
1. Simple
2. Compound
3. Compound-complex
4. Complex

Lesson 1, pages 269-272
Activity A
1. whenever he can
2. If he gets up early
3. because he enjoys it
4. Unless it is raining hard

Activity B
1. team / practiced - Simple
2. practice / is; players / are - Complex
3. team / begins - Simple
4. they / do warm up; injuries / are - Complex
5. team / practices - Simple
6. it / rains; team / can practice - Complex
7. Baseball / is played - Simple

Activity C
1. than any other dog
2. than anyone else does
3. than Sue
4. than the others
5. as she can be

Lesson Review
Part A
1. since she was born
2. Because Angela became Sue's friend
3. if he tries
4. than English is
5. when she is with Sue

Part B (the verb is in bold print)
1. We **will go**; when summer **arrives**
2. Cliff **bought**; because he **needed** transportation
3. (You) **get**; if you **are**

4. <u>No one</u> **can run**; than <u>Rick</u> (**can run**)
5. <u>Rick</u> **can hit**; than <u>anyone</u> on the team **can (hit)**

Part C

1. simple
2. complex
3. simple
4. complex
5. complex

Lesson 2, pages 273-277
Activity A

1. that my answer; direct object
2. what Angela would say; direct object
3. Who will be first; subject
4. who should go first; object of preposition
5. what I want; predicate noun
6. what the score is; direct object

Activity B

1. who
2. who
3. who
4. whom
5. whom

Activity C

1. (who) found my book

2. ((that)) you lost

3. (What) I need right now

4. (whoever) finds my book

5. ((that)) Shelly has my book now

Activity D

1. object of preposition
2. direct object
3. predicate nominative
4. What you see — subject;
   what you get — predicate nominative
5. direct object

Activity E

1. "All the world's a stage"; line
2. that he would win the race; hope
3. that the world was round; idea
4. which gave women the right to vote; amendment
5. thirty-first president, Herbert Hoover

6. that the earth revolved around the sun; discovery
7. which is a list of books; bibliography

Lesson Review

1. whatever we needed; object of preposition
2. that you can diagram this sentence; direct object
3. that love conquers all; appositive
4. what I need; predicate nominative
5. (that) she's tired; direct object
6. When the paper is due; subject
7. Where he was going; subject
8. where he was going; direct object
9. what he needs; predicate nominative
10. whoever asked him; object of preposition
11. that he could win the contest; appositive
12. what you pay for; direct object
13. what the dog brought home; predicate nominative
14. where he put his book; direct object
15. who is coming; direct object
16. How Sue did the job; subject
17. What she will do next; direct object

Lesson 3, pages 279-281
Activity A

1. whom I know
2. that Shelly gave Ralph
3. that she gave
4. who sits in the first seat
5. that is guaranteed for one year

Activity B

1. (that) Shelly belongs to

2. (that) someone organized

3. (whose) name is Mr. Smith

4. (that) he had trained

5. (that) he directed

Activity C
Answers will vary.

Lesson Review
Part A
1. that come in a box; potato chips
2. who gave the party; people
3. who plays right field; one
4. who drove the bus; man
5. that Sue wore to the party; dress
6. who was in line behind me; girl
7. who lived next door; man
8. who starred in that movie; one
9. that was about the Civil War; book
10. that had three bedrooms; apartment

Part B
1. compound
2. complex
3. complex
4. simple
5. complex

Lesson 4, pages 282-286
Activity A
1. complex
2. compound-complex
3. compound
4. complex
5. compound-complex

Activity B
1. Richard Wright worked as a dishwasher.
2. Richard Wright
3. worked
4. intransitive (no object)
5. as, preposition; a, adjective; dishwasher, noun
6. Richard Wright
7. when?
8. who, subject; was born, verb
9. he, subject; became, linking verb
10. became; an author is the predicate noun and completes the idea

Activity C
1. Answer may vary.
2. Ralph also has a part-time job.
3. Noun (appositive)

Activity D
Answers may vary.

Activity E
1. complex sentence with an adverb clause
2. compound-complex sentence with an adverb clause
3. complex sentence with a noun clause as the predicate noun
4. complex sentence with an adjective clause describing Mrs. King
5. complex sentence with a noun clause as direct object

Activity F
Answers will vary.

Lesson Review
1. complex
2. simple
3. compound-complex
4. compound
5. complex

Chapter Review
Part A
1. clause
2. prepositional phrase
3. prepositional phrase
4. clause
5. clause
6. prepositional phrase
7. clause
8. prepositional phrase

Part B
1. adjective (describes person); noun (direct object)
2. adjective (describes Ralph); adjective (describes present)
3. adverb (tells when)
4. noun (object of preposition)
5. noun (subject)
6. adverb (tells why)
7. adverb (tells why); noun (object of verb knows)

Part C
1. The gift is a record album.
2. gift, subject; is, linking verb; album, predicate noun
3. that Mrs. King bought for the first guest
4. Mrs. King, subject; bought, verb
5. adjective; it describes gift
6. complex (one independent and one dependent clause)
7. statement

Part D
1. simple
2. compound
3. complex
4. compound-complex
5. simple (shoes)

Chapter 14
The Verbal and the Verbal Phrase

Overview

Chapter 14 explains the verbal and the verbal phrase and their roles in sentences. The lessons will help students recognize infinitives, gerunds, and participles in sentences as well as to recognize the role verbals play in forming sentence patterns.

Chapter Goals

At the conclusion of the chapter, students are expected to:
- locate verbals in sentences and to identify them as either infinitives, gerunds, or participles;
- locate verbal phrases in sentences and identify them as either infinitive, gerund, or participial phrases.

Vocabulary

adjective	infinitive
adverb	participle
gerund	participial phrase
identify (6)	scholarship (5)

Teaching Suggestions

1. Review the definitions of the grammatical terms in the vocabulary.
2. Stress that verbals are verb forms used as other parts of speech in a sentence. For example, an infinitive is used as a noun; therefore, it may be a subject, a direct object, an object of a preposition, or any other part of a sentence that requires a noun.

Lesson 1. Infinitives and Infinitive Phrases
Overview

The activities in Lesson 1 are designed to help students identify infinitives and infinitive phrases in sentences. Students are expected to recognize the part of the sentence pattern played by the infinitive.

Lesson Goal

At the conclusion of Lesson 1, students are expected to recognize infinitive phrases in sentences.

Vocabulary

ambition(6)	equipment (5)
analyze (8)	infinitive
attempt (5)	prepositional phrase
cole slaw	tense (6)
diagram (6)	

Teaching Suggestions

1. Review the vocabulary words and discuss the lesson objective.
2. Throughout the lesson activities, ask students to identify the sentence patterns and to determine whether the sentences are simple, complex, compound, or compound-complex.
3. Ask students to locate the verb or verb phrase in each clause. Be sure they understand the difference between the verb, which expresses an action or state-of-being related to the subject, and a verbal.
   Example: I like to run.
   To run is the name of something I like. It does not tell what the subject is doing.

Follow-Up Activity

Select a passage from a literature book, magazine, or newspaper and have students locate infinitives. The following verbs are often completed with infinitives without *to*: bid, dare, feel, let, make, observe, see, watch. Example: I heard the man *laugh* at you.

Lesson 2. Gerunds and Gerund Phrases
Overview

Students learn to recognize the gerund used as a subject, direct object, or other noun element.

Lesson Goal

At the conclusion of the lesson, students are expected to locate gerund phrases in sentences.

Vocabulary

architect (6)	gerund
cheating (5)	haystack
complement (10)	motorcycle
diagram (6)	pleasure (5)

Teaching Suggestions
1. Discuss the vocabulary words and the lesson objective.
2. Review verb phrases using the progressive verb form:

> He is riding a bike.
> She *was walking* to school.

Compare the present progressive with the gerund and point out that a gerund is the present participle form of the verb. What makes it a gerund is the way it is used in a sentence. A gerund names an action and appears in the sentence as a subject, a direct object, or some other part that requires a noun.

> *Walking* is good exercise.
> *Riding* a bike is fun.

3. Throughout the lesson, ask students to locate the verb or verb phrase in each sentence as well as the gerunds and gerund phrases.

Follow-Up Activity
Have the students make a list of ten verbs ending in *-ing*. Then, tell them to use the words in a sentence as gerunds. Tell them to identify the part of the sentence pattern each gerund is. Next, tell them to use the same words as part of verb phrases in ten other sentences.

Lesson 3. Participles and Participial Phrases
Overview
In Lesson 3, students learn to recognize participles and participial phrases in sentences. The location of the participle is explained. Students identify participles used as regular modifiers as well as those used in the predicate adjective position.

Lesson Goal
At the conclusion of the lesson, students are expected to recognize participles and participial phrases in sentences.

Vocabulary
participial   pitiful (7)
participle   snack (6)

Teaching Suggestions
1. Explain that the word participle is a noun. It is the name of a kind of word. The word *participial* is the adjective form of the word. A *participial phrase* is a kind of phrase.
2. Review the other vocabulary words and the lesson objective.
3. Explain that a participle is a verb form. It is either present (ending in *-ing*), or past (usually ending in *-ed*). Review the irregular verbs in Chapter 4.
4. A participle can only be distinguished from a gerund or from a word that is part of a verb phrase by the way it is used in a sentence. For example:

Singing *is* fun. (gerund — subject)
We bought a *singing* teakettle. (participle — adjective)
They *are singing.* (part of the verb phrase)
Another example that may be used to demonstrate the distinction is:
A *watched* pot never boils. (participle — adjective)
We *are watching* the pot. (verb phrase)
We *have watched* the pot all day. (verb phrase)

Follow-Up Activity
Have the class make a list of verbs ending in *-ing*. Students should make up three sentences with each word, using each as a gerund, a participle, and then as a present or past progressive verb phrase.

Chapter Review
Before beginning the Chapter Review, conduct any Follow-Up activities previously omitted as well as the suggested review activities below.

Vocabulary
diploma (8)
graduation (6)
graduating (6)

Review Activities
1. Use the Lesson Review activities from Chapter 14. Have students locate the verbals and verbal phrases, identify the kind of each verbal, and identify the role each verbal plays in the sentence.

2. Select a passage from a literature book, magazine, or newspaper and have the students search for verbals and verbal phrases. They should identify the type of verbal and the function each has in the sentence. Students should also be asked to identify the verb in each clause in the sentence.

Answer Key to Chapter 14
Warm-Up A
1. smiling
2. running
3. to read
4. torn
5. to buy

Warm-Up B
1. to find a job - Infinitive Phrase
2. winning the contest - Participial Phrase
3. Their celebrating - Gerund Phrase
4. To be a good musician - Infinitive Phrase
5. to play baseball - Infinitive Phrase
6. Winning the games - Gerund Phrase
7. to win a scholarship - Infinitive Phrase
8. standing on the field - Participial Phrase

Lesson 1, pages 291-295
Activity A
1. to use
2. to fish
3. to catch
4. to fry
5. to make
6. to make

Activity B
1. to the lake - Prepositional Phrase
   to fish - Infinitive
2. to the boat - Prepositional Phrase
3. to begin - Infinitive
4. to catch - Infinitive
5. to beat - Infinitive
   to Louis - Prepositional Phrase
6. to have caught - Infinitive
7. to the other boater - Prepositional Phrase
8. to another boat - Prepositional Phrase
9. to reel - Infinitive
10. to fry - Infinitive

Activity C
1. Noun (Subject)
2. Noun (Predicate Noun)
3. Noun (Direct object)

4. Adjective (Modifies *attempts*)
5. Adverb
6. Adverb (Modifies *hard*)
7. Adverb (Modifies *fun*)
8. Noun (Object of preposition)

Activity D
      inf. d.o. adv. ph.
1. to reel the fish into the boat

      inf. adv.
2. to fight hard

      inf. adv. adv. ph.
3. to get free from the hook

      inf. d.o. adv. ph.
4. to bring it into the boat

      inf. d.o.
5. to help him

      inf.   d.o.
6. To land that fish

Activity E
1. help
2. cheer
3. see
4. hold
5. smile

Activity F
1. to catch - adjective (Modifies *turn*)
2. to reel - noun (Direct Object)
3. to get - adverb (Modifies *tried*)
4. to pull - predicate adjective
5. To catch - noun (Subject)

Lesson Review
1. to be home by dark
2. to stop at six o'clock
3. to count the fish
4. to catch many fish
5. To catch enough fish for dinner
6. to eat
7. to feed your family and mine
8. to fry this one
9. (to) get; to go home
10. to leave

Lesson 2, pages 296-298
Activity A
1. Riding
2. jogging
3. playing
4. barking

Activity B
1. running of the Boston Marathon - Direct Object
2. Winning that race - Subject
3. thinking about it - Direct Object
4. having his own marathon in Hanover - Object of a Preposition
5. finding joggers - Direct Object
6. Setting up the race - Subject
7. running and winning - Appositive

Lesson Review
1. Flying an airplane
2. Reading books
3. swimming in the lake
4. planning buildings
5. chasing cats
6. singing and dancing
7. cooking / cleaning up
8. Finding gerunds
9. Locating a needle
10. growing food
11. Knowing you
12. weeding their gardens
13. Planning our vacation
14. fishing for trout
15. reading

Lesson 3, pages 299-301
Activity A
1. Adjective
2. Verb
3. Verb
4. Adjective
5. Adjective
6. Verb

Activity B
1. Howling wildly - wind
2. sitting in the first row - girl
3. Expecting the worst - Louis
4. locked inside the car - keys
5. Reading her book intently - Mrs. Agnello

6. addressed to the bank - letter
7. Recommended by his teachers - Bobby
8. cooked by Dana - dinner
9. looking from the top of the building - Barbara

Activity C
1. Walking to school - we
2. Speaking in front of the class - Bobby
3. needed for the party - thing
4. Lost - kittens
5. Swimming at the beach - we frightened - we (Pred. Adjective)

Activity D
1. Fishing - gerund
   to do - infinitive
2. singing - participle
3. Finding - gerund
   to do - infinitive

Lesson Review
1. running around the track (boy)
2. lost (dog)
3. Rowing rapidly (We)
4. broken (bike)
5. Standing on the corner (we)
6. Arriving early (we)

Chapter Review
Part A
1. graduating - gerund
2. to see - infinitive
3. Smiling - participle
4. walking - participle
5. to leave - infinitive
6. to have - infinitive

Part B
1. Standing in front of the school for a last look - Participial Phrase
2. Graduating from high school - Gerund Phrase
3. to catch a last look at her school - Infinitive Phrase
4. Shutting her eyes - Participial Phrase
5. to celebrate the graduation - Infinitive Phrase

Student Workbook
Answer Key

Page 5, Find the Nouns
1. Mrs. Parham, George, politeness
2. Cindy, family, Kansas
3. Jose, book, couch
4. audience, violinist
5. soldier, medal. bravery
6. horse, fence
7. crowd, game, pleasure
8. Yoshi, mother, car
9. hikers, Blueberry Mountain
10. Henry, newspaper, porch
11. price, coat
12. Walter, knowledge, Baseball
13. waters, Long Pond, sunlight
14. Mr. Wilson, idea, party
15. Alice, dictionary, shelf
16. The Doors, group
17. John Adams, president
18. Cora, dream, cat
19. Peter, ring, stone
20. speed, Tom, race

Page 6, Finding Common and Proper Nouns
Answers will vary.

Page 7, Finding the Plural Form
1.	boxes	9.	ladies
2.	boys	10.	men
3.	calves	11.	mice
4.	children	12.	shelves
5.	chiefs	13.	spies
6.	geese	14.	teeth
7.	keys	15.	wives
8.	knives	16.	women

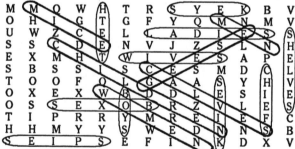

Page 8, Selecting the Correct Possessive Form
1.	trees	9.	hikers'
2.	team's	10.	books'
3.	fire's	11.	men's
4.	plant's	12.	snake's
5.	band's	13.	friend's
6.	children's	14.	Jean's
7.	cats'	15.	coach's
8.	mouse's		

Page 9, Using Nouns Correctly
1.	York City	6.	City Music Hall
2.	brother	7.	zoo
3.	city's	8.	men's

4. Building   9. Janet's
5. tickets   10. leaves

Page 10, Singular and Plural Pronouns
1. They - P
2. It - S; our - P
3. Those - P; my - S
4. My - S; his - S
5. that - P
6. you - S, P; your - S,P
7. he - S; we - P; them - P
8. Our - P
9. he - S; them - P
10. they - P; ours - P
11. this - S; your - P, S
12. That - S; my - S; he - S
13. Somebody - S; her - S
14. Us - P
15. He - S; nobody - S
16. All - P
17. herself - S
18. My - S; us - P; we - P
19. we - P; ourselves - P
20. her - S

Page 11, Selecting the Correct Pronoun
1. "May he have a sandwich?" he asked.
2. "Here are my books," said Janet.
   "Where are yours?" Janet said to Ted.
3. "I want you to help," she said to him.
4. I put my papers right here. Have you seen them?
5. "I invited him for dinner," Ted said to Janet.
6. "We are hungry," said Ted.
7. "This is my chair; that one is hers," said Ted.
8. "We are happy that you could have dinner with us," said Janet.

Page 12, Find the Pronouns and Their Antecedents
1. Tina...she
2. Terry and Paul...their
3. me...Sue
4. I...Mrs. Parsons
5. Ellen...she
6. vase...it
7. Pam...she
8. boys...they
9. Lucy...she; pin...it
10. Lee...his
11. I...Joe; you...Bob
12. Mrs. Carson...she
13. It...game
14. Mr. Wardrop...his
15. We...Meg and Sally
16. house...that
17. Larry...he; boy...whom
18. day...it
19. cat...which
20. Tony...he

Page 13, Finding Pronouns
1. I, personal; nothing, indefinite
2. Who, interrogative; your, personal

3. This, demonstrative
4. that, relative
5. whom, relative; I, personal
6. few, indefinite
7. which, interrogative; you, personal
8. none, indefinite
9. Those, demonstrative
10. that, relative; one, indefinite
11. some, indefinite
12. what, interrogative; your, personal
13. him, personal
14. Who, interrogative
15. several, indefinite; us, personal
16. who, relative

Page 14, Using Pronouns Correctly
1. who
2. her
3. no errors
4. whose
5. Which
6. It's
7. my
8. We
9. that
10. those
11. its

Page 15, Finding Adjectives
her
television
cable
their
the
cable
free
the
company's
a
television
the

exciting
the
television
That
first
the
the
the
heavy
the
difficult
a

good
their
the
finished
the
cable
The
their
the
free
access

Page 16, Find the Adjectives
1. a, big - garden; this - year
2. her, French - class
3. Ted's car; a, good - radio
4. the - winter
5. American - literature
6. his - money's; money's - worth
7. Ted's, full - refrigerator
8. Sixteen - people; the - party
9. Most - people; vanilla - ice cream
10. Last - Sunday; the, football - game
11. That, chocolate, good - cake
12. friendly - I
13. those, two, larger - buildings
14. The - Wildcats; their, first - game; last - Saturday
15. a, shooting - star
16. a - pencil
17. Several, late - people
18. Andy's, interesting, hard - class
19. The, gold, expensive - chain
20. his, final - decision

Page 17, Proper Adjectives
1. Swiss
2. Rehoboth Beach
3. German
4. Spanish
5. European

Students will use Swiss, French, Democratic, Shakespearean, and Spanish in sentences.

Page 18, Comparisons with Adjectives
1. positive
2. comparative
3. comparative
4. comparative
5. superlative
6. superlative
7. superlative
8. comparative
9. comparative
10. positive
11. comparative
12. positive, comparative
13 superlative
14. positive
15. superlative
16. superlative
17. comparative
18. comparative
19. positive
20. comparative

Page 19, Words of Power
1. A   3. B   5. A   7. C   9. A
2. B   4. C   6. A   8. A   10. A

Page 20, Verbs and Helping Verbs
1. been
2. does
3. Has
4. is
5. is
6. has
7. doing
8. did
9. were
10. done
11. is
12. done
13. did
14. be
15. Has
16. had
17. having
18. doing
19. been
20. Are

Page 21, Verb Phrases
1. was spent
2. died
3. had studied
4. lived
5. would build
6. was surveying
7. began
8. went
9. caught
10. had
11. died
12. had willed
13. started
14. had sent
15. was engaged
16. married

Page 22, Irregular Verb Forms
1. writing
2. found
3. ridden
4. had
5. grown
6. wrote
7. broken
8. made
9. making
10. done
11. spoke
12. made
13. taken
14. bought
15. written
16. found
17. rides
18. breaks

Page 23, The Irregular Be Verbs
1. is
2. was
3. was
4. were
5. is
6. been
7. is
8. is
9. is
10. were
11. is
12. is
13. been
14. is
15. is
16. is
17. were

Page 24, Active and Passive Verbs
1. passive
2. active
3. passive
4. passive
5. passive
6. active
7. passive
8. active
9. passive
10. active
11. active
12. passive
13. passive
14. passive
15. active
16. active
17. active
18. passive
19. passive
20. active

Page 25, Rename the Subject
1. Dawn - subject; was - linking verb; friend - predicate noun
2. Adverbs, adjectives - subjects; are - linking verb; parts - predicate noun
3. Pat - subject; is - linking verb; athlete - predicate noun
4. C-SPAN - subject; is - linking verb; station - predicate noun
5. Princeton - subject; is - linking verb; university - predicate noun

6. marigold - subject; is - linking verb; flower - predicate noun
7. birthday - subject; is - linking verb; event - predicate noun
8. car - subject; is - linking verb; Toyota - predicate noun
9. dessert - subject; is - linking verb; strawberries - predicate noun
10. apple - subject; is - linking verb; snack - predicate noun

Answers may vary. Suggested answers are given:
1. network
2. capital
3. movie
4. musician
5. President
6. fruits
7. vegetables
8. kinds
9. movie, book
10. parties

Page 26, Find the Linking Verb
1. is	6. are	11. feel	16. smelled
2. is	7. feel	12. appeared	17. looked
3. are	8. smells	13. seemed	18. remained
4. were	9. Have felt	14. felt	19. looks
5. Have felt	10. appear	15. felt	20. seem

Page 27, Action or Being
1. being	6. being	11. being	16. being
2. action	7. action	12. action	17. action
3. action	8. being	13. being	18. being
4. being	9. action	14. action	19. action
5. being	10. action	15. being	20. being

Page 28, Describe the Subject
Answers may vary. Suggested answers are given.
1. friendly
2. spicy
3. clean
4. terrific
5. expensive
6. tall, handsome
7. slender
8. crunchy
9. well
10. juicier

Page 29, Adverbs Answer Questions
1. never
2. loudly; yesterday
3. again; just
4. quickly; sometimes
5. comfortably; now
6. carefully; weekly
7. there
8. upstairs; usually

Page 30, Finding Adverbs
1. softly
2. extremely
3. quietly
4. often
5. well
6. here
7. not
8. finally
9. unusually
10. happily
11. very, gracefully
12. too, lightly
13. suddenly
14. breathlessly
15. not
16. crossly
17. almost
18. never
19. not, now
20. quite, fast

Page 31, Adverbs and Adjectives
1. adverb	8. adjective	15. adjective
2. adjective	9. adjective	16. adjective
3. adverb	10. adverb	17. adjective
4. adverb	11. adverb	18. adverb
5. adjective	12. adjective	19. adjective
6. adverb	13. adjective	20. adverb
7. adverb	14. adverb	21. adjective

Page 32, Add an Adverb
Answers will vary.

Page 33, Choosing the Correct Adverb
1. gave	6. comes	11. will be
2. will arrive	7. will sing	12. agreed
3. will visit	8. is	13. go or will go
4. fix	9. is	14. has been
5. enjoy	10. sent	15. trim

Page 34, Prepositional Phrases as Modifiers
1. tournament - in England
2. Most - of the world's best players
3. boy - from West Germany
   man - to win the tournament
4. kind - of racket
5. All - of his matches
   matches - in the tournament
6. play - by Boris Becker
7. Many - of his points
8. courts - with their grass surfaces
9. man - with a powerful serve
10. boy - with the smile
    smile - on his face
11. player - with red hair
12. finals - on center court
    court - at Wimbledon, England

Page 35, Adding Prepositional Phrases
Answers will vary.

Page 36, Preposition or Adverb?
1. preposition	6. preposition	11. preposition
2. adverb	7. adverb	12. adverb
3. adverb	8. preposition	13. preposition
4. preposition	9. adverb	14. adverb
5. adverb	10. preposition	15. preposition

Page 37, Prepositional Phrases
1. with chocolate sauce - adjective
2. on the tree - adjective
3. with Victor - adjective
4. of the students - adjective
   in the fall - adverb
5. in school - adverb
6. on his hamburgers - adverb
7. at the end - adjective
   of the line - adjective
8. After the party - adverb
   with Ted - adverb
9. to the game - adverb
   on Saturday - adjective
10. in our garden - adjective
11. with cream and sugar - adjective
12. with Janet - adverb
    for new shoes - adverb
13. on Friday - adjective
14. around the corner - adverb
15. with the white markings - adjective

Page 38, Prepositions and Their Objects
1. to - Bob	11. around - room
2. on - rug	12. over - creek
3. with - friend	13. from - me
4. near - mountain	14. Above - fireplace
5. for - Rick	15. into - ocean
6. on - porch	16. off - shelf
7. down - hill	17. behind - door; for - boots

8. of - hers
9. in - town
10. about - flags

18. In - minutes
19. over - bridge; past - woods
20. with - friends; at - movies

3. no
4. no
5. yes

8. no
9. no
10. yes

13. no
14. yes
15. yes

Page 39, The Right Connections

1. My favorite baseball players are Hank Aaron and Reggie Jackson.
2. John Steinbeck wrote *The Red Pony* and *The Grapes of Wrath*.
3. My garden has zinnias, marigolds, and weeds.
4. For the picnic, we bought hot dogs and rolls.
5. Betty likes hot dogs, but not hamburgers.
6. This soda is sugar-free and caffeine-free.
7. My older brother, Casey, and my little brother, Jimmy, play soccer.
8. I have two poodles named Velvet and Coco.
9. Velvet is black, and Coco is champagne.
10. Our telephone is touch-tone and yellow.

Page 40, Finding Conjunctions

1. Unless; subordinating
2. Either...or; correlative
3. however; coordinating
4. when; subordinating
5. since; subordinating
6. whether...or; correlative
7. and; coordinating
8. as well as; coordinating
9. Whenever; subordinating
10. but; coordinating
11. Because; subordinating
12. but; coordinating
13. and; coordinating
14. or; coordinating

Page 41, Punctuating With Conjunctions

1. home, it
2. beans, carrots, and
3. movie, but
4. chicken; also, she
5. hurry, we
6. busy; moreover, she
7. flute, piano, and
8. now, or
9. began, the
10. lunch, I
11. snows, Tina
12. sheep, a goat, and some
13. airport, for
14. well; therefore, they
15. fell, we
16. quiet, for

Page 42, Using Interjections

Answers may vary. Suggested answers are given.
1. goodness,
2. what! Who
3. Well,
4. Stop!
5. Wow, what ...gift! It's
6. Brr,
7. Ummmm,
8. Oh, no,
9. Hurry,
10. Oh,
11. Nonsense! You
12. Hello,
13. Hey! Is
14. Alas,
15. Oh, woe is me,
16. Oh, boy,

Page 43, Words of Feeling

Answers will vary. Suggested answers are given.
A. 1. Wow! I need help.
2. Hey, you are late!
3. Oh, I am so happy!
4. Boy! I love your new car.
5. Hurrah! Our team won the game.
B. 1. Oh, boy! That was fun.
2. Whew! I am tired.
3. Hey, buddy! You're in my way.
4. Wow! What a great hit.
5. Ha! Ha! That's too funny!

Page 44, Expressing a Complete Idea

1. no
2. yes
6. yes
7. yes
11. yes
12. yes

Page 45, Purposes of Sentences

1. ? question
2. . statement
3. ? question
4. . request
5. ? question
6. . or ! command
7. . statement
8. ? question
9. . request
10. . or ! command
11. . statement
12. ? question
13. . or ! command
14. . request
15. . or ! command
16. . statement

Page 46, Finding Subjects

1. Soap operas
2. People
3. Many of the sponsors
4. daytime dramas
5. One famous soap opera
6. Your grandmother
7. Another...in the 1940s
8. My father's favorite
9. *One Man's Family*
10. It
11. That program
12. people
13. You
14. The soap opera stars
15. People

Page 47, A Sentence Has Two Parts

The subject of each sentence is given here. The rest of the sentence is the predicate.
1. All of the students
2. Victor, (you)
3. (You)
4. The lady ... the line
5. Everyone
6. No one
7. The whole class
8. The best hitter on the team
9. Both Sue and Janet
10. Spring and fall
11. Darleen's dog, Tiny
12. Twelve ... chip cookies
13. any one of you
14. it
15. my gloves

Page 48, Interrogative Sentences

1. you - subject; Have seen Billy - predicate
2. Who - subject; is that - predicate
3. that - subject; Isn't the new puppy's name - predicate
4. your friend - subject; Will be staying for lunch - predicate
5. anyone in this house - subject; has seen my other tennis shoe- predicate
6. you - subject; Do think the puppy dragged it under the sofa again - predicate
7. you - subject; Why don't ask the dog - pred.
8. you - subject; Can't ever give me a straight answer - predicate
9. this - subject; Is your shoe - predicate
10. I - subject; How can ever thank you - predicate

Page 49, Compound and Simple Sentences

1. S
2. C
3. C
4. S
5. S
6. C
7. C
8. S
9. S
10. C
11. S
12. S
13. S
14. C
15. C

Page 50, Transitive and Intransitive Verbs

1. fell; intransitive
2. cheered; intransitive
3. Stop; transitive
4. should see; transitive
5. will win; transitive
6. laughed; transitive
7. Write; transitive
8. named; transitive
11. Have read; transitive
12. Spend; transitive
13. left; intransitive
14. will stay; intransitive
15. listened; intransitive
16. Have seen; transitive
17. is; intransitive
18. rode; transitive

9. Give; transitive
10. made; transitive
19. is walking; intransitive
20. give; transitive

Page 51, Understanding Intransitive Verbs

1. being
2. being
3. active
4. active
5. being
6. active
7. being
8. being
9. being
10. active
11. being
12. active
13. active
14. being
15. active

Page 52, Sentences to Diagram

1.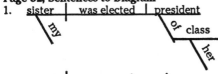

2.

3.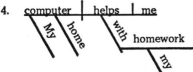

4.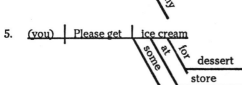

5.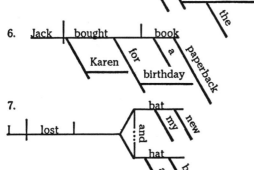

6.

7.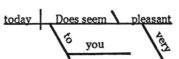

Page 53, Complements of Linking Verbs

1. pleased; adjective
2. cook; noun
3. big; adjective
4. friendly; adjective
5. ready; adjective
6. difficult; adjective
7. nice; adjective
8. beige; adjective
9. cheerleader; noun
10. enthusiastic; adjective
11. president; noun
12. James Madison; noun
13. name; noun
14. Dolley Madison; noun
15. book; noun

Page 54, Linking Verbs: Yes or No?

1. no - are going
2. no - graduated
3. yes - was
4. yes - feels
5. no - named
6. no - won
7. yes - became
8. yes - is
9. yes - was
10. no - watched
11. yes - looks
12. no - have

Page 55, Object or Predicate Noun?

1. predicate noun
2. direct object
3. direct object
4. predicate noun
5. predicate noun
6. direct object
7. predicate noun
8. predicate noun
9. predicate noun
10. direct object
11. predicate noun
12. direct object

Page 56, Sentences to Diagram

1. Hamlet - subject; is - linking verb; play - noun

2. weather - subject; is - linking verb; hot and humid - adjective

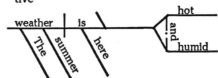

3. today - subject; does seem - linking verb; pleasant - adjective

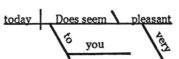

4. Maryland - subject; is - linking verb; state - noun

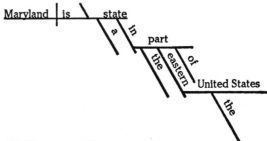

Page 57, Phrases and Clauses

1. prepositional phrase
2. dependent clause
3. dependent clause; independent clause
4. prepositional phrase
5. dependent clause; independent clause
6. prepositional phrase
7. prepositional phrase; prepositional phrase; independent clause
8. dependent clause
9. independent clause; dependent clause

10. dependent clause
11. prepositional phrase
12. dependent clause
13. dependent clause, independent clause
14. dependent clause
15. prepositional phrase

Page 58, Finding Dependent Clauses
1. when it rains
2. Before James arrived
3. that she would be late
4. the party was nice
5. that come in a can
6. Because ... high school
7. after he jogs
8. who visited us last week
9. What I said
10. what she said
11. Whoever is hungry
12. if you want to
13. Because it rained
14. who moved to Cleveland
15. who live in that house

Page 59, Dependent Clauses
1. noun: what I need
2. adverb: because we were hungry
3. noun: whoever finds the clues
4. adjective: that was his favorite
5. noun: whom she did not know
6. noun: what you said
7. adjective: that has a hole in it
8. adverb: whenever he has time
9. adjective: that escaped from the zoo
10. adverb: wherever Megan goes
11. noun: whose garden is so beautiful
12. adjective: which Robert hoped to buy
13. adverb: whenever you have time
14. adjective: that is gray and white
15. noun: that a hurricane is coming

Page 60, Find the Dependent Clause
1. adjective clause, adjective clause
2. adverb clause, adjective clause
3. adverb clause
4. adverb clause
5. noun clause
6. adverb clause
7. noun clause
8. adjective clause, adverb clause
9. adverb clause, adjective clause
10. adjective clause, adverb clause

Page 61, Infinitive Phrases
1. to sit - infinitive; on the beach - prepositional phrase
2. to see - infinitive; dolphins - direct object

3. to count - infinitive; them - direct object
4. to walk - infinitive; on the beach - prepositional phrase
5. to get - infinitive; sunburn - direct object
6. to prevent - infinitive; burn - direct object
7. to fish - infinitive; for flounder - prepositional phrase
8. to eat - infinitive; flounder - direct object
9. to clean - infinitive; fish - direct object
10. to solve - infinitive; today - adverb
11. to be - infinitive; on the beach - prepositional phrase
12. to walk - infinitive; barefooted - adjective; in the sand - prepositional phrase
13. to feel - infinitive; breeze - direct object
14. to decide - infinitive; on a restaurant - prepositional phrase
15. to taste - infinitive; good - predicate adverb

Page 62, Recognizing Infinitives
1. prepositional phrase
2. infinitive
3. infinitive
4. infinitive
5. prepositional phrase
6. prepositional phrase
7. infinitive
8. infinitive
9. infinitive
10. infinitive
11. infinitive
12. infinitive
13. infinitive

Page 63, Find the Verbals
1. infinitive - to work-out
2. infinitive - to watch
3. gerund - Hitting
4. gerund - Listening
5. gerund - Relaxing
6. gerund - Weightlifting
7. participle - weightlifting
8. infinitive - to go
9. gerund - Working
10. participle - needed
11. gerund - snacking
12. participle - stewing
13. infinitive - to stew
14. infinitive - to improve
15. gerund - writing

Page 64, Three Kinds of Verbals
Exercise 1:
1. to use the boat
2. to have steak for dinner
3. to eat
4. to leap to the next tree
5. To join the country club

Exercise 2:
1. Barking
2. Finding the right house
3. swimming
4. Camping
5. racing

Exercise 3:
1. broken
2. Fixing the bike ourselves
3. riding the bike
4. Shouting happily
5. squeaking loudly again